NEW PERSPECTIVES
ON ANCIENT JUDAISM

Studies in Judaism

NEW PERSPECTIVES
ON ANCIENT JUDAISM

VOLUME FOUR

THE LITERATURE OF EARLY RABBINIC JUDAISM:
ISSUES IN TALMUDIC REDACTION AND INTERPRETATION

Senior Editors

Jacob Neusner   Ernest S. Frerichs

William Scott Green   Gary Porton

Editors

Alan J. Avery-Peck   Roger Brooks

Paul Virgil McCracken Flesher (Managing Editor)

Volume Editor
Alan J. Avery-Peck

UNIVERSITY
PRESS OF
AMERICA

Lanham • New York • London

Copyright © 1989 by

University Press of America,® Inc.

4720 Boston Way
Lanham, MD 20706

3 Henrietta Street
London WC2E 8LU England

Library of Congress Cataloging-in-Publication Data

The Literature of early Rabbinic Judaism : issues in Talmudic
redaction and interpretation / volume editor, Alan J. Avery-Peck ;
senior editors, Jacob Neusner ... [et al.] ; editors, Alan J. Avery
-Peck, Roger Brooks.
    p.   cm.
(New perspectives on ancient Judaism ; v. 4)
(Studies in Judaism)
Includes bibliographical references and indexes.
1. Talmud--Criticism, Redaction. 2. Rabbinical literature-
-History and criticism. I. Avery-Peck, Alan J. (Alan Jeffery),
    1953–   II. Series. III. Series: Studies in Judaism.
    BM177.N485   1989   vol. 4   88–22501 CIP
[BM500.2]
296'.09'01 s--dc19
[296.1'2066]
ISBN 0–8191–7179–4 (alk. paper)

All University Press of America books are produced on acid-free paper.
The paper used in this publication meets the minimum requirements of American
National Standard for Information Sciences—Permanence of Paper for Printed Library
Materials, ANSI Z39.48–1984.   ∞

for
Gary Porton

Contents

Part One
Recent Studies in Talmudic Redaction

Part Two
The Systemic Interpretation of Rabbinic Documents

Part Three
Early Judaism in Its Graeco-Roman Context

Preface

The essays collected in this volume address three central questions in the contemporary study of early Rabbinic Judaism: how the canonical texts of Talmudic Judaism reached their present formulation (Part One); what approaches are appropriate in reading and analyzing those texts (Part Two); and what insights can be gained by reading those texts in light of the evidence of the world contemporary to their authors (Part Three). While covering a diverse range of specific issues and documents, the volume as a whole is intended, therefore, to comprise a cogent statement of the current state of the field of early Rabbinic studies. Let me explain.

The single most significant factor that distinguishes contemporary study of Rabbinic literature and religion from traditional study is the recent scholarship's rejection of the long held assumption that the texts of Judaism come to us as historical documents, accurately portraying events as they occurred, accurately transmitting statements as they were said, and accurately describing a single, ongoing religion and communal structure, a Judaism that was practiced just as the Rabbis describe.

The essays in this volume typify contemporary research in early Rabbinic literature in that, rejecting the earlier consensus, they recognize that these documents speak for editors and redactors who created of diverse antecedent traditions the cogent documentary statements presently before us. These papers accordingly pose questions designed, on the one hand, to reveal the social and religious worlds of those authorships, or, on the other, to clarify the character of the redactional process itself, so as to make possible the recovery of the meaning of the antecedent materials from which the later redactors created their literatures.

In Part One, on the redaction of the Babylonian Talmud, Martin Jaffee, Richard Kalmin, David Kraemer and Avram Reisner take up different aspects of the redactional question: To what extent was the redaction of the Babylonian Talmud influenced by the existing model of the Talmud Yerushalmi (Jaffee)? When did the process of Talmudic redaction begin to take place (Kalmin)? By what process was Talmudic argumentation preserved (Kraemer)? And how were these sources used in the creation of extended ("contrived") Talmudic pericopae (Reisner)? Michael Chernick's paper, an overview of the state of the field, responds to the preceding three essays, putting this recent work in the perspective of larger trends in the study of Talmudic redaction and setting the agenda for future study. What is clear is that, only when we properly comprehend the processes through which Talmudic dicta were preserved and edited can the Talmud serve to answer historical questions concerning the development of Rabbinic Judaism in the third through sixth centuries.

The contemporary recognition of the significance of redactors and formulators, who took up and transmitted in new forms and to particular purposes statements and ideas of earlier masters, leads to a second approach to the documents of Rabbinic Judaism. This approach examines the canonical documents of Rabbinic Judaism viewed as redacted wholes, so as to determine the ideologies that informed their authorships. In line with this approach, the essays in Part Two ask what we learn by addressing the individual documents of Rabbinic Judaism as complete, systematic statements of their redactors, who used inherited traditions to express their own particular world view and social and religious attitudes.

While taking up diverse documents and issues, these essays accordingly share the notion that the documents before us reflect the ideologies of their individual authorships, not of some undifferentiated, monolithic "Judaism." This notion is explained in Jacob Neusner's paper, which proposes use of the topic of economics in order to gain insights into the distinct systems of Judaism represented in different historical periods and contexts. Neusner rejects the prevalent notion that there is a single economics of *Judaism*, insisting instead that economists' questions must be applied to distinct *Judaisms*, in order to reveal the character of each system in its own context. This same notion, that individual documents of Judaism speak for an authorship and, through their details, reveal a larger world view, informs the work of Paul Flesher, on the Mishnaic concept of the slave, and of Irving Mandelbaum, on the conception of the relationship between the people of Israel and God expressed in the laws of diverse-kinds.

As a unit, these three papers represent perhaps the most important trend in the contemporary reading of Rabbinic documents. Together, they argue that Judaism in antiquity never was a seamless whole, to be studied directly through an analysis of facts of history, theology and the like. The *Judaisms* of late antiquity, rather, are presented to us only through literary remains. These Judaisms must be revealed, accordingly, through a careful reading and interpretation of distinct documents, which are the consciously created products of individual authorships, each with its own world view and approach to the traditions it inherited.

In Part Three, Sandra Shimoff's essay discusses the relationship between the ideology of nascent Rabbinic Judaism and the social attitudes of the Graeco-Roman world in which that Judaism grew. By locating within the Graeco-Roman world the source of the Rabbinic literature's negative attitude towards shepherds, this paper illustrates the significant understandings to be gained by reading Rabbinic writings in light of their context within the Graeco-Roman world. Turning away from the particular interest in Rabbinic Judaism that marks the other essays in this volume, Dixon Slingerland takes up an important historical question concerning the Jews in the Graeco-Roman world. A careful evaluation of Suetonius's reference, in Claudius 25.4, to Claudius's expulsion of the Jews from Rome shows that the passage points to a significant occurrence within the history of early Roman Jewry. This essay thereby sets the stage for important research into the conditions under which Jews lived outside of the land of Israel at the start of the Rabbinic period.

It is my hope that this volume will facilitate the reader's acquiring more than simply a knowledge of the particular topics and important issues discussed in these papers. Rather, addressed to specialists in the fields of literary, historical and religious studies, as well as to those who focus upon the study of early Rabbinic Judaism, it intends to make clear the vibrancy of Rabbinic studies as a facet of contemporary critical scholarship. For as is clear throughout these papers, both the methods employed in and the insights produced through the study of early Rabbinic Judaism derive from the humanistic disciplines of today's university.

Except for Chapter Six, the essays collected here originated in the History and Literature of Early Rabbinic Judaism Section of the Society of Biblical Literature, which I have had the honor of chairing since 1984. The essays that comprise Chapters II-V were delivered at the annual meeting of the Society held in Anaheim, California, in 1985. Chapters I and VII-X were on the program of the annual meeting in Boston in 1987. On behalf of all of the authors, I express thanks to the Society for the opportunity it provides for the discussion of central issues in contemporary Rabbinic studies and offer my gratitude to all of the participants in our section meetings, whose many insights are found on the pages of this volume.

I am grateful for the support of the David and Bea Herman Fund, which underwrote the costs of preparing the copy for this volume. Established within the framework of the Tulane University Jewish Studies Program, the fund was created by Shael and Helen Herman, Avram and Mollie Herman, Mark Herman, and Sherill and Ralph Zatzkis in honor of their parents, Mr. and Mrs. David Herman, of New Orleans, Louisiana. I am pleased to join the Herman family in celebrating their father's seventy-fifth birthday, on which this book is dated, and in recognizing their parents' dedication to values central in the Jewish tradition: love of family, learning, and Torah.

Mr. Shael Herman kindly took time from his legal practice and his own scholarly endeavors in order to assist in the proofreading of this volume. I appreciate the many corrections and suggestions he offered. I am, as always, grateful for his assistance and for the support he continues to offer on a wide range of projects. I am pleased to recognize as well the support of Tulane University's Committee on Research, whose grant of a research fellowship during the summer of 1988 facilitated my editing of this volume.

I am thankful to my teacher, Professor Jacob Neusner, for his generous counsel in the preparation of this book and for his making possible its publication in the Studies in Judaism series, of which he is Editor in Chief. With great pleasure I acknowledge his help and advice, from which I continually benefit.

Gary Porton, to whom this volume is dedicated, was my undergraduate teacher at the University of Illinois, Urbana. I am grateful for the efforts he took to introduce me as an undergraduate to the contemporary study of Judaism, and I am thankful for the support and friendship he has continued to offer throughout my career.

New Orleans, Louisiana   Alan J. Avery-Peck
May 18, 1988

Abbreviations

Arakh.	= Arakhin		Orl.	= Orlah
A.Z.	= Abodah Zarah		PAAJR	= Procedings of the American Academy for Jewish Research
B.	= Babylonian Talmud			
Ber.	= Berakhot		Pes.	= Pesahim
Bes.	= Besah		Qoh.	= Proverbs
B.K.	= Baba Kamma		R.	= Rabbi
B.M.	= Baba Metzia		R.H.	= Rosh Hashanah
Dt.	= Deuteronomy		San.	= Sanhedrin
Eruv.	= Eruvin		Shab.	= Shabbat
Ex.	= Exodus		Shev.	= Shevuot
Gen.	= Genesis		Sot.	= Sotah
Git.	= Gittin		Suk.	= Sukkah
Hag.	= Hagigah		T.	= Tosefta
Hal.	= Hallah		Taan.	= Taanit
Hor.	= Horayot		Y.	= Yerushalmi, the Palestinian Talmud
Hul.	= Hullin			
JQR	= Jewish Quarterly Review		Yeb.	= Yebamot
Ket.	= Ketubot		Zeb.	= Zebahim
Ki.	= Kings		Zuck.	= Zuckermandel, Moses Samuel, *Tosefta, Based on the Erfurt and Vienna Codices, with Parallels and Variants* (Trier, 1881-82; revised edition with supplement by Saul Lieberman, Jerusalem, reprint: 1970).
Kil.	= Kilaim			
Lev.	= Leviticus			
M.	= Mishnah			
Mak.	= Makkot			
Men.	= Menahot			
Neg.	= Negaim			
Nid.	= Niddah			
Nu.	= Numbers			

TRANSLITERATIONS

א	=	'		ל	=	l
ב	=	b		מ,ס	=	m
ג	=	g		ן,נ	=	n
ד	=	d		ס	=	s
ה	=	h		ע	=	c
ו	=	w		ף,פ	=	p
ז	=	z		צ	=	ṣ
ח	=	ḥ		ק	=	q
ט	=	ṭ		ר	=	r
י	=	y		ש	=	š
ך,כ	=	k		שׁ	=	ś
			ת	=	t	

Part One

RECENT STUDIES IN TALMUDIC REDACTION

Chapter One

The Babylonian Appropriation of the Talmud Yerushalmi: Redactional Studies in the Horayot Tractates

Martin S. Jaffee
University of Washington

Introduction

The question of the impact of the fourth-century Palestinian Talmud upon the sixth-century Talmud of Babylonia[1] has a history extending back to the late Geonic reconstructions of the course of Rabbinic tradition. In the closing years of the Babylonian Geonate one first finds the assertion that the redactors of the Bavli knew the earlier work and took full account of its discussions in the production of their own final and authoritative document.[2] This claim, while not

---

[1] The date of the Bavli's redaction is somewhat of a chimera, insofar as the Talmud's text seems to have undergone amplification well into the Geonic period (see D. Goodblatt, "The Babylonian Talmud," in J. Neusner, *The Study of Ancient Judaism. II. The Palestinian and Babylonian Talmuds* [New York: 1981], p. 314). Nevertheless, the first quarter of the sixth century has much to recommend it as a likely context for a substantial editorial effort to collate Babylonian learning in documentary form. See the recent discussion of R. Kalmin, "The Post-Rav Ashi Amoraim: Transition or Continuity? A Study of the Role of the Final Generations of Amoraim in the Redaction of the Talmud," *AJS Review* XI:2 (1986), pp. 158-163.

[2] The key source is the comment of the eleventh-century Moroccan codifier, Isaac Alfasi, at the end of his examination of the halakhic material in Bavli Erubin (ed. Romm, 35b). As translated by S. Baron, *A Social and Religious History of the Jews*, vol VI (Philadelphia: 1958), p. 25, Alfasi states of the Bavli: "We have to rely on our Talmud, for it is the younger one. *[The Babylonian Sages] were more familiar with the western [Palestinian] Talmud than we are*, and they would not have rejected any of its statements, unless they were sure that it was not dependable" (emphasis supplied). Ginzberg (*A Commentary on the Palestinian Talmud* [Hebrew], vol. I [New York: 1941; repr. 1971], pp. 83-90), has shown that Alfasi's view is grounded either in faulty interpretation or faulty texts of the responsa of Hai Gaon. At issue for Hai, as for earlier polemicists on behalf of the Bavli such as Yehudai Gaon or Sherira Gaon, is not the extent to which the Yerushalmi was known in Babylonia, but simply the greater reliability of Babylonian tradition over that of Palestine. Nevertheless, Alfasi's understanding of the Geonic material has served as the point of departure for most modern students of the problem until Ginzberg.

3

implausible on its face, has been almost unanimously discounted by the major voices in the past generation of critical Talmudic scholarship.[3]

Two quite independent grounds for dismissal are usually proposed. First, while the Bavli clearly contains many passages paralleled in the Yerushalmi, and

---

[3]Extensive bibliographical references may be consulted in B. Bokser, "An Annotated Bibliographical Guide to the Study of the Palestinian Talmud" in J. Neusner, op. cit., pp. 187-191, D. Goodblatt, op. cit., p. 288 and J. Davis, "Bibliography" in J. Neusner, *Judaism: The Classical Statement. The Evidence of the Bavli* (Chicago: 1986), pp. 244-245. Cf. H.L. Strack/G. Stemberger, eds., *Einleitung in Talmud und Midrasch*, 7th ed. (Munich: 1982), pp. 193-194.

The most vigorous recent assertion of this thesis comes from an unlikely quarter. Jacob Neusner, who has otherwise reduced to rubble much of the wissenschaftliche edifice of Talmudic studies, has devoted a monograph (*The Bavli and Its Sources: The Question of Tradition in the Case of Tractate Sukkah* [Atlanta: 1987]) to the question of the relation between the two Talmuds. Here he argues that, while the Bavli may share sources with the Yerushalmi, it is "an autonomous document, disconnected from and unlike its predecessor in all the ways that matter" (p. 53). This conclusion, however, is grounded in precisely the sorts of literary comparisons which, as I indicate in the present paper, most obscure our ability to see commonalities of redactional structure linking the two documents. See in particular pp. 30-53 where Neusner demonstrates beyond doubt that the formulators of Babylonian units of Mishnaic exegesis refer hardly at all to earlier materials presently found in the Yerushalmi. His commitment to the autonomy of the Bavli, however, leads him to overlook his own indications of shared patterns of redaction in chapter one of Y./B. Sukkah (ibid., pp. 26-30).

Neusner's support of the modern consensus on the relations between the two Talmuds stems, ironically, from his well-taken charge that in most matters modern Talmudic scholarship has ignored the genuine distinctions of literary style and worldview reflected in the diverse Rabbinic corpus. In the present case, however, his zealousness in probing the diversity of Rabbinic literature results in a tendency to draw too stark a distinction between what he calls "traditional" modes of transmitting learning and purely rational, systematic inquiry. For Neusner, these can hardly coexist (ibid., p. 1). It is not self-evident, however, that independence of judgment and vision, such as that exercised by the Bavli in its exegesis of the Mishnah, is incompatible with immersion in traditional processes of learning. An apt metaphor, supplied by Neusner himself, makes the point: "...the Bavli presents its own message, a systemic statement of an original character, much as in reshaping and reconstituting received conventions, the composer or artist accomplishes something fundamentally original" (p. 52). To my knowledge, few in the post-Romantic ethos of our own day would care to argue that artistic originality can proceed outside of some nurturing tradition received from the past. To the degree, then, that originality is itself bound up with tradition, there is no irreconcilable conflict between them. The Bavli can indeed be "original" while at the same time being largely dependent, as I argue, on an earlier work for its power of originality.

frequently cites traditions ascribed to Palestinian scholars,[4] it never quotes the earlier Talmud by name as a source. Nor, for the most part, does it indicate through techniques such as citation formulae that it has appropriated and built upon literary materials now found in the Yerushalmi. Second, the claim that the editors of the Babylonian Talmud knew and used the Yerushalmi serves an obvious polemical agenda, to promote the Babylonian recension of Rabbinic learning as the authoritative voice in the consolidation of Rabbinic Judaism within the domains of Islam and Christendom.[5]

In neither case, however, are the grounds for dismissal of such arguments especially convincing. In response to the observation that the Bavli fails to cite or otherwise employ the Yerushalmi in its own discussions, one might point out that there is no particular reason to expect it to do so. While the Bavli shows intense interest in all materials bearing the imprimatur of Rabbinic authority, it assumes that only Tannaitic materials enjoy a privileged status as *sources* of tradition. Quite properly, it reserves its distinctive citation formulae for these alone,[6] finding no occasion to develop a system of citation for post-Tannaitic materials (other than the ubiquitous "Rabbi X said...."). Finally, in regard to the point that the claim of Babylonian knowledge of the Yerushalmi serves a polemical purpose, one may simply observe that not all polemics need necessarily be false.

In addition to these simple criticisms of the assumptions underlying the present consensus, yet another can be added. To claim the essential independence of the two Talmuds leaves unexplained a most peculiar state of affairs. As matters now stand, one must believe that the sixth-century editors of the Bavli were virtually ignorant of a document which precedes them by well over a century and entirely anticipates their own work in form, scope and conception.

It is, of course, possible that literary innovations, as other cultural innovations, may occur in close chronological sequence yet independently of any

---

[4]W. Bacher, *Tradition und Tradenten in den Schulen Palaestinas und Babyloniens* (Leipzig: 1914; repr. Berlin: 1966), pp. 506-523, lists tradents responsible for bringing Amoraic traditions from Palestine to Babylonia. A typology of reports of Palestinian learning is offered in J.N. Epstein, *Introduction to Amoraitic Literature* [Hebrew] (Jerusalem: 1962), pp. 293-312. One such report, in the name of Abba Mari, is preserved in B. Hor. 13a, ls. 17-18, and confirmed in Y. Horayot 48a, ls. 38-39.

[5]See, for example, Ginzberg, op. cit., Baron, op. cit., pp. 16-27 and note 16, pp. 327-328 and E.Z. Melammed, *An Introduction to Talmudic Literature* [Hebrew] (Jerusalem: 1963), pp. 555-558.

[6]See J.N. Epstein, *Introduction to the Text of the Mishnah* [Hebrew], 2nd ed. (Jerusalem and Tel Aviv: 1964), pp. 803-897.

causal nexus. But this is hardly likely to be the case in Rabbinic culture, whose representatives appear to have maintained strong avenues of communication throughout the Amoraic period.[7] In sum, the present scholarly consensus regarding the independence of the Bavli from the Yerushalmi, while nearly universal and grounded in the work of the most important representatives of critical Talmudic research, seems for all that no more plausible than the polemics of the Bavli's original apologists.

In light of this state of affairs, the present study reopens the question of Babylonian knowledge and use of the Talmud Yerushalmi. It presents, in particular, the results of a comparative study of tractate Horayot in each Talmud.[8] At the core of the study is a shift in the method of literary analysis most commonly used in the comparative study of Rabbinic texts. Instead of comparing discrete literary units in each tractate, a method which usually reveals how little Babylonian discussions genuinely depend upon or appropriate the results of earlier analogous materials in the Yerushalmi, the present study focuses upon the larger patterns in the redactors' work within each tractate.[9] I shall argue that the appropriation of the Palestinian Talmud by the Bavli's editors becomes clear, not at the level of individual textual parallels, but rather at the level of literary craft and organization, as large sequences of discourse are

---

[7] See Bacher, cited in note 4 above, and ibid., pp. 475-505, where Babylonian materials known to the Yerushalmi are listed. For general accounts of intellectual interchange between Palestinian and Babylonian Amoraim, see A. Steinsaltz, "Relations Between Babylonia and the Land of Israel" [Hebrew], *Talpiyot* 9 (1964), pp. 294-306 and J. Schwartz, "Tension Between Palestinian Scholars and Babylonian Olim in Amoraic Palestine," *Journal for the Study of Judaism* 11 (1980), pp. 78-94.

[8] The basis for this study is in M. Jaffee, *The Talmud of Babylonia, An American Translation. XXVI. Tractate Horayot* (Atlanta: 1987), pp. 43-45, n. 6. The present essay amplifies and refines the impressions reported in that preliminary discussion.

[9] It is of utmost importance to clarify the senses in which I use the term "redaction" and "redactors". Following most recent literary historians of the Talmud (see Goodblatt, op. cit., pp. 314-318), I distinguish the Amoraic redaction of discrete units of literary discourse, which can have occurred throughout the fourth and fifth centuries without reference to the Talmud Yerushalmi, from the post-Amoraic organization of collections of such units into series of discourses redacted for association with a given pericope of the Mishnah. While it is possible that later redactors made their presence felt in previously-edited materials as they prepared them for use in larger constructions and new contexts, it is still important to distinguish the two activities. It is only the circle responsible for the final organizational patterns of the Talmud's Amoraic sources which, I hold, makes use of the extant version of the Talmud Yerushalmi.

redacted in each gemara around the core of the same Mishnaic tractate. Here there is suggestive evidence that the Yerushalmi, in more or less its extant form, shapes the Babylonians' conception of their own task and, morever, supplies the dominant exegetical themes appropriated by them for amplification or revision.

The Evidence of Tradition-Historical Analysis

Before moving to the evidence of Bavli Horayot's appropriation of its predecessor, it may be useful to show how tradition-historical analysis in the Horayot tractates only confirms the established view that the Bavli proceeds in nearly total ignorance of the Yerushalmi. The present exercise, then, while lengthy, is crucial to the larger point of this experiment. It clarifies the extent to which the key assumption of earlier scholars—that literary relationships can only be demonstrated at the level of discrete units of textual tradition—has obscured the ways in which the editors of the Bavli make use of the Yerushalmi.

Exclusive of purely thematic analogues, which shall occupy us much later, there are some 33 clear textual correspondences in the two Horayot tractates. By "textual correspondences" I mean cross-documentary units of text which intersect in one of three ways.[10] In the first type of correspondence, two separate units in each tractate cite a common Tannaitic text and develop it in thematically similar ways. Thus the correspondence is constituted by the selection of an authoritative citation and a clear decision in each Talmud to develop its import along similar lines. The second type of correspondence may be identified where a shared

---

[10]I identify 14 such passages. Throughout this essay, as in the following list, I identify these passages by page and line numbers as well as the opening and closing words of the Yerushalmi, ed. Krotoschin, and the Bavli, ed. Romm.

1. 45d, 20-29 (R 'YMY-ŠM'L)/2b, 10-21 (KGWN-ḤKMYM)

2. 46a, 27-34 (WL'-HKNSH)/4a, 43-55 (TNN-ŠRY')

3. 46a, 36-40 (R BWN-GWP)/4b, 13-26 (BᶜY-MYNḤ)

4. 46b, 7-12 (TNY-HŠBTYM)/5b, 26-29 ('MRY-PR)

5. 46b, 15-23 (R M'YR-ṢYBWR)/5a-b, 17-12 (T"R-MᶜYNY)

6. 46b, 23-25 (M'N-B'YN)/3b, 42-45 ('MR-B'YN)

7. 46b, 46-53 (R ZᶜYR'-HHWT'YN)/6a, 40-43 (T"R-PṬWRYN)

8. 46c, 15-28 (NPŠ-MWRYN)/6b-7b, 34-1 (ŠWGG-ŠNYHN)

9. 46c, 47-52 (R YRMYH-BKLL)/7b, 42-45 (W'YLW-LH')

10. 47b, 59-63 ('KL-HŠLYŠY)/11a, 24-43 (Bᶜ-TYQW)

11. 47c. 21-29 ('MR-HZH)/10b, 2-28 (T"R-HZH)

12. 47c, 29-33 (MLK)-('WTH)/11a-b, 57-7 (T"R-LDYDHW)

13. 47d, 56-59 (HW'-KN)/12b, 40 (W'ḤR-WHW')

14. 48a-b, 70-69 (ᶜD-HBRYWT)/13a-b, 24-1 (T"R-GYYṢY)

Amoraic pericope, usually of a forensic character, plays a role in two larger discussions in each tractate.[11] A third comes into view where, in each Horayot, two discussions routinely employ common Tannaitic citations along with common versions of accompanying Amoraic discussions.[12] Any of these types of correspondence raises the possibility of the Bavli's dependence upon its Palestinian predecessor. Yet such dependence is most difficult to prove on the basis of tradition-historical analysis. Space permits discussion of only one example of each type of apparent correspondence.

We begin with the first of our three types, in which each Talmud cites and develops the same Tannaitic text in its discussion of a given Mishnaic passage. Indications that the Bavli knew the Palestinian discussion in its present form would lie in the former's exploitation of the latter's exegetical results for its own purposes. This is precisely the kind of relationship, however, which is most difficult to identify with certainty.

---

[11]The 12 passages are as follows:

1. 45d, 14-15 ('YN-BD')/2a, 10-12 ('MR-'TM); cf. 21-22

2. 45d, 31-35 (HBRYY'-HT'WT)/2a, 41-46 (BPLWGT'-HT)

3. 45d, 17-20/56-61 ('"R MN'-B"D)/3b, 2-4 ('MR-KWLN)

4. 45d-46a, 74-10 (TWLDWT-PTWRYN)/3a, 40-41 ('YB^CY'-MSTRP)

5. 46a, 16-22 (RBY-^CMW)/3a, 33-36 ('MR-QHL)

6. 46a, 23-27 (R HZQYH-LYSYQH)/4a, 31-34 (T"L-MSWT)

7. 46a, 45-49 (KTYB-WMYNW)/4b, 40-42 (WHT'M-LK)

8. 46d, 43-45 (R YWSY-'HRT)/9a, 12-15 (TNY'-LW)

9. 46d, 55-65 (KYNY-BHWS)/9b, 5-14 ('MR-QHL)

10. 46d, 66-73 ('"R-S^CYRH)/9b, 15-22 ('"R-PTWR)

11. 47a, 57-58 (HBRYY'-MBYNYHWN)/11a, 18-20 (HNYH'-LMYMR)

12. 48a, 38-39 ('"R-HSR)/13a, 17-18 ('MRY-KTYB)

[12]The seven passages are as follows:

1. 45d, 33-51 (WQSY'-QYWM)/2b, 25-44 ('MR-RWBW)

2. 46a, 63-72 (SBT-BNYMN)/5a, 44-45 (M'T-B"D); cf. 5b, 43-44 ('L'-'HRYN')

3. 46b, 34-38 (RBY-HYTH)/5b-6a, 46-40 (TNY'-HYTH)

4. 46c, 60-67 (R 'WMR-M^CYNY)/8a, 17-45 (MNLN-Q"ML)

5. 46d, 36-43 ('"R-MBY'H)/8b-9a, 40-12 ('MR-DGZ')

6. 47c, 68-74 (TNY-S'YR)/12a, 47-51 (T"R-Q"ML)

7. 47d, 66-75 (R L^CZR-SPH)/12b, 46-53 ('MR-BHD')

Two representative discussions appear at Y. 47c, ls.29-33 and B. 11a-b, ls. 57-7, both redacted with M. 3:3.[13] The Mishnah offers a subtle exegetical transformation of Lev. 4:22ff., which holds that the tribal chieftain (NŚY') of the wildernesss period is required to offer a bull in expiation of inadvertent transgressions of certain divine prohibitions. In the Mishnaic rendering the term NŚY' is extended to include the historically quite distinct office of the king (MLK):

> Who is called the Ruler (NŚY')?   This is the King.
>
> For it is said: (WHEN THE RULER SINS...) WITH REGARD TO ONE OF ALL THE COMMANDMENTS OF THE LORD HIS GOD (Lev. 4:22)—[this refers to a leader] above whom there is none save THE LORD HIS GOD.

Scripture's procedure for the atonement of a tribal head in the wilderness sanctuary, then, is now applicable to the monarch, who pursues his atonement in the Temple.

While the Mishnah seems clearly to have in mind a Davidide making his atonement in the Jerusalem Temple, the Yerushalmi explores the possibility that the Mishnaic extension of Scripture's meaning might even include non-Davidides ruling over the northern kingdom of Israel (i.e. Samaria):

> A. 1. A King of Israel and a King of Judah—they are both equal.
>
> 2. This one is not greater than that, nor is that one greater than this.
>
> B. Now what is the Scriptural proof of this? NOW THE KING OF ISRAEL AND...THE KING OF JUDAH WERE SITTING ON THEIR THRONES...AT THE THRESHING FLOOR...(1 Ki. 22:10). The phrase AT THE THRESHING FLOOR means "as if on the threshing floor" [implying that neither was elevated above the other].
>
> C. Said R. Yose b. R. Bun: And this [equivalence in status] applied only until the time of Jehu b. Nimshi.
>
> D. Now what is the Scriptural proof of this? AND THE LORD SAID TO JEHU, ... "YOUR SONS OF THE FOURTH GENERATION SHALL SIT ON THE THRONE OF ISRAEL" (2 Ki.10:30). Yet from then on [his successors] would seize [the throne] like bandits.

---

[13]Here and in the appendix I use the enumeration of Mishnaic pericopae found in the Yerushalmi, ed. Krotoschin.

The Tannatic citation (A), focusing upon the equality of the two dynasties, implies in the present context of redaction that each king is obliged to engage in the atonement procedures mandated at Lev. 4:22ff. The key point is at C-D. From the death of Jehu, the Samarian kings were regarded as illegitimate and so are disqualified from the procedure, which continued to be incumbent upon the Davidic heir in Jerusalem until the destruction of the Solomonic Temple. In relation to M. 3:3, then, the Yerushalmi implies that the King in question is, from the time of Jehu's reign onward, solely the Davidide presiding over the Kingdom of Judah.

Turning to the comparable discussion in the Babylonian Horayot (11a-b), we find a rather different set of interests:

A'. Our Rabbis taught:

1.WHEN THE RULER SINS (Lev. 4:22)—is it possible [that this includes only a] tribal chief, such as Nahshon b. Aminadav?

{2.   ...deletion...}

3. [No,] just as elsewhere [Scripture refers to the King as one] above whom there is none save THE LORD HIS GOD (Dt. 17:19), so too here the Ruler [is one] above whom there is none save THE LORD HIS GOD (Lev. 4:22) (Sifra Hovah, par. 5:1; cf. T. Hor. 2:2).

B'. Rabbi inquired of R. Hiyya: For one such as myself, what is the ruling? [If the Temple were standing would I make my atonement] with a male goat [as does the Ruler or King]?

C'. He said: Really! [How can this verse apply to you as long as] your rival [the Exilarch] is in Babylonia?

D'. He retorted: The kings of Israel and the kings of the House of David—these bring their own [offerings] and those bring their own (cf. T. Hor. 2:2).

E'. [R. Hiyya] said: That applied [when the kings of Israel and Judah] were not subordinate to each other. But now we [in the Patriarchal administration of the Land of Israel] are subordinate to them [in the Babylonian Exilarchate].

The Bavli's point of departure is Sifra (A'), which repeats and amplifies the Mishnah's exegetical demonstration that only Rulers from the wilderness and monarchical periods bring expiation offerings. This supplies an introduction of sorts to the independent dialogue of B'-E', which asks if the patriarchal title, NSY', permits the holder to regard himself as carrying on the divinely appointed Scriptural office with all its attendant duties and privileges. The answer, E', is entirely in line with the Mishnah's own view that the laws of expiation have no practical application following the destruction of the Solomonic Temple.

Clearly, the literary relationship between the Palestinian and Babylonian discussions is slender indeed. The only point of apparent congruence, the Tannaitic citations at Yerushalmi A and Bavli D', is in fact illusory, for the Bavli's version of T. Hor. 2:2 bears only a vague thematic correspondence to the Yerushalmi's source. In all other matters of Mishnaic exegesis, the units pursue their own interests in independent ways, agreeing only that one must in some way delimit the precise range of the Mishnaic extension of the wilderness rite into later Israelite institutions. The Bavli not only fails to develop the issues of the Yerushalmi; it shows no awareness of them at all.[14]

We move now to the second type of textual correspondence common in our tractates, that in which a single discussion of Amoraic origin serves as the shared ground of two larger literary constructions. The example before us, correlated with M. 2:8, appears at Y. 46d, ls. 55-64 and B. 9b, ls. 5-14. The Mishnah states:

> [As for transgressions which involve] heeding the call to testify, or for uttering vain oaths, or for contaminating the Sanctuary and its holy things...the individual, the Ruler and the Anointed [Priest] are obliged [for an offering of variable value].
>
> Nevertheless, the High Priest[15] is not obliged for contamination of the Sanctuary and its holy things—the words of R. Simeon.

The offering of variable value, prescribed at Lev. 5:1ff. for a variety of errors of ommission and commission, is an expiation offering (of grain, birds, small or large cattle), the value of which is linked to the economic status of the expiant. The Mishnaic dispute concerns an unclear point in Scripture regarding who in

---

[14]Nevertheless, the Bavli's interest in the Patriarch's relation to the ancient modes of Israelite leadership does have a *thematic* analogue at Y. 47c, 39-56. At issue there is whether a NSY' who has been punished by stripes can be returned to his office or whether, to the contrary, his "descent in holiness" has permanently impaired his capacity to return to his earlier status. There follows a narrative in which Judah the Patriarch, apparently under the assumption that the Sages mean their ruling to apply to his Patriarchate, threatens Simeon b. Laqish, who holds that the NSY' can indeed be beaten while in office.

[15]KHN GDWL: so most MSS. and editions in contrast to the Romm edition's conflate reading, MŠYḤ KHN GDWL. See R. Rabbinowicz, *Sefer Diqduqei Soferim* (Repr. Jerusalem: 1960), vol. XIII, p. 26, line 9.

fact is obliged to bring the offering. As we might expect, both Talmuds are interested in the grounds upon which Simeon exempts the Anointed in particular from the need for expiation if he has inadvertently contaminated the sanctified area of the Sanctuary.

The Yerushalmi opens its inquiry as follows:

A. This is [the proper reading of] the Mishnah:

1. **But the High Priest is not obliged [for an offering of variable value] for contamination of the Sanctuary and its holy things—the words of all [authorities].**

2. **And the Ruler [is free of obligation] for [his lapse in] heeding the call to testify—the words of R. Simeon.**

This textual emendation involves a transposition and revision of views assigned in the Mishnah; Simeon's Mishnaic opinion is now assigned to Sages as a normative ruling (A.1), while the Mishnah's obligation of the Ruler for an offering is restated as an exemption and re-assigned to Simeon. The Yerushalmi, unfortunately, offers no explanation of what is at stake in this revision. Its real interest lies in explaining the view now assigned, at A.1, to the scholarly consensus:

B. Said R. Yohanan: [Sages' view is based upon the following—] NEITHER SHALL HE [i.e., the Anointed Priest] GO OUT OF THE SANCTUARY NOR PROFANE IT (Lev. 21:12). Thus, if he does go out, he does not profane it!

C. R. Yoshaiah, R. Yonah, R. Bun b. Kahana objected: But it is written: A WIDOW, A DIVORCEE, ONE WHO HAS BEEN DEFILED AND A WHORE— THESE SHALL HE NOT TAKE (Lev. 21:14). Therefore, if he does take her, he has not committed a profanation?

D. [Well, if Sages' view is based upon such fragile exegetical grounds,] what then?

E. Said[16] Hezekiah: [Sages' view is explained as follows:] THAT SOUL SHALL BE EXTIRPATED FROM AMONG THE COMMUNITY [SINCE HE HAS DEFILED THE SANCTUARY] (Num. 19:20). [Thus, extirpation is reserved for] one whose offering [for contamination of the Sanctuary] is identical to that of the community [for which a male goat atones (Lev. 16:3ff.)].

[16']MR. The version of Yerushalmi Horayot published in ed. Romm of the Bavli as a substitute for the missing "Tosafot" (16a) reads: TNY, as if Hezekiah's pericope were a Tannaitic source.   Although, as Lieberman has shown ("Yerushalmi Horayot" [Hebrew], *Festschrift for R. Hanokh Albeck* [Jerusalem: 1963], pp. 283-305), this text contains many superior readings, the present is clearly not among them.

This excludes the Anointed, since his offering [of a bull] is not identical to that of the community.

F. They responded: But indeed the Ruler [who in the Mishnah is obliged for the present offering]—his offering [of a male goat in expiation of inadvertent transgressions] is not identical to that of the community [which offers a bull]!

G. [To this apparent contradiction, Hezekiah replied:] But it is identical on the Day of Atonement [since the Ruler atones with the community].

H. [They responded:] But indeed his fellow priests—[their offerings of the bull] are not identical [to that of the community] on the Day of Atonement!

I. [He replied:] They are identical the rest of the year [during which they atone for communal transgressions with a bull along with the rest of Israel].

The structure of the discussion is simple. B's explanation of A.1 is shown at C to be absurd. This prepares us for Hezekiah's more subtle exegetical defense (E), grounded in the contrast between the atonement offerings of the Anointed and the other members of the community. The debate at F-G+H-I spells out the comprehensive scope of Hezekiah's opinion which, in the end, proves the cogency of A.1's revision of M. 2:8.

If we compare now the Babylonian version of this discussion, we will be struck both by the remarkable similarities of textual detail as well as the way redactional decisions have thoroughly transformed the meaning of the parallel material. In its opening discussion of the Mishnah, B. 9b begins:

A'. Said Hezekiah: What is the Scriptural proof for the view of R. Simeon?

For it is written: THEN THAT PERSON SHALL BE EXTIRPATED FROM AMONG THE COMMUNITY (Num. 19:20). [Thus exirpation is reserved for] one whose offering is identical to that of the community.

[It follows that] this one [i.e., the Anointed Priest] is excluded, since his offering [of a bull on the Day of Atonement] is not identical to that of the community.

B'. If so, the Ruler also [should be exempt, for] his offering is not identical to that of the community!

C'. [Not at all, for] as far as expiation on the Day of Atonement is concerned, [his offering] is identical [to that of the community].

D'. If so, the [common] priests also [should be exempt, for] their offerings are not identical to that of the community for expiation on the Day of Atonement!

E'. [This is irrelevant, for] the priests are identical to the community regarding the rest of the commandments during the entire year.

F'. [This is just the point, for] the Anointed is indeed identical [to the community] regarding the rest of the commandments during the year [for he, like the community, atones with a bull]!

G'. [Then why is he exempt from the offering of variable value?] Rather, said Rava [in defense of Hezekiah]: Put it this way—[this offering of variable value is brought only by] one whose pollution offering [for inadvertent transgression] is identical to that of [common] individuals.

And who is this? The community![17]

Clearly enough, A'-E' follows with great fidelity the debate preserved in the Yerushalmi at E-I, while F'-G' contributes an expansionary gloss. Do we, then, find evidence that the Bavli has accepted and built upon exegetical results achieved in the present version of the Yerushalmi?

Not at all. Recall the language with which the Bavli's Hezekiah begins his exegesis: "What are the grounds for the view of R. Simeon?" The Bavli's exercise in Mishnaic exegesis ignores the fact that, in the Yerushalmi, Hezekiah's exegetical energies are mounted *not in explanation of the Mishnah, but in revision of it*. Shared by the two tractates, then, is a nearly identical debate between Hezekiah and his colleagues. Each tractate, however, creates for the debate an entirely independent context reflective of its own assumptions about the soundness of the Mishnaic text. In sum, the Bavli's use of Hezekiah's material in no way presupposes the present use to which the Yerushalmi puts it.

We turn, finally, to an example of the third type of literary correspondence found in the Horayot tractates. Here pericopae of both Tannaitic and Amoraic origin are taken in each tractate as the basis for a larger exegetical discussion of a single Mishnah. At issue in the present example (Y. 47d, ls. 66-75/B. 12b, ls. 46-53) is the clarification of the claim (M. 3:6) that, because of his enhanced status of holiness, the High Priest in mourning performs rites distinctive to his own status, while common priests perform mourning rites appropriate to non-priestly Israelites. Specifically, the High Priest tears his garment "at the bottom" while others do so "at the top".

The first order of business, in each Talmud, is to clarify the Mishnah's description of the mourning ritual. The Yerushalmi's discussion opens as follows:

---

[17]That is, in the event that the community transgresses without judicial directions, it makes atonement as a collection of mere individuals, each person offering a female animal. Since the Anointed always atones with a bull, he is excluded from liability for an offering of variable value, as Hezekiah has argued.

A. R. Leazar in the name of Kahana: **At the top** (M. 3:6)—this means he tears the garment above the stiff border; **at the bottom** means he tears beneath the stiff border.

B. R. Yohanan says: This literally means the bottom [of the garment].

Compare now this dispute about the meaning of the Mishnah's prescription with the version of the Bavli:

A'. Said Rav: **At the bottom** (M. 3:6) literally means the bottom [of the garment]. **At the top** literally means at the top.

B'. But Samuel said: **At the bottom** means he tears the garment beneath the stiff border. **At the top** means he tears above the stiff border.

C'. And both terms are used in reference to the collar.

There can be little doubt that before us is a Babylonian recension of a Palestinian pericope. First, third-century Palestinian authorities have been replaced by Babylonian contemporaries of Palestinian origin with whom each is elsewhere associated.[18] Second, the Babylonian reversal of the opinions meets the redactional needs of the Bavli's editors, who routinely record disputes between Rav and Samuel with the latter's view in the final position.[19] Further, Rav's version of Yohanan's position is amplified so that it provides a perfect formal balance to the contrasting view of Leazar/Samuel. Finally, a gloss (C') clarifies precisely which portion of the priestly garment is under discussion at B', a matter left unclear not only in the Mishnah, but in the Yerushalmi as well.

Have we, then, found a case in which the Bavli clearly depends upon and amplifies a completed discussion of Yerushalmi Horayot? Before making a judgment we must examine the ways in which this pericope is subjected to exegesis in each tractate. As we shall see, it becomes very difficult indeed to argue that the editors of the completed Babylonian unit might have used something like the completed Palestinian counterpart in their own work.

The Yerushalmi continues:

C. R. Yohanan went up to vist R. Hanina. While on the way, he heard that the other had died. He sent word to bring him his best Sabbath garments. Then he tore them.

---

[18]See, for example, H. Albeck, *Introduction to the Talmud Babli and Yerushalmi* [Hebrew], 2nd printing (Tel Aviv: 1975), pp. 170-173.

[19]See B. Bokser, *Samuel's Commentary on the Mishnah* (Leiden: 1975) and idem., *Post Mishnaic Judaism in Transition* (Chico: 1980) for a full discussion of the literary traits of Samuel's traditions.

D. R. Yohanan differs from R. Judah in two matters and the view of R. Leazar in the name of Kahana concurs with that of R. Judah.

E.   If [R. Yohanan, who tore his garment in mourning for a non-relative,] concurs with R. Judah, he shouldn't have rent his garment at all!

F.   And this [view of R. Leazar in the name of Kahana] is relevant only where his father or mother is concerned, as in the view of R. Meir.

G.   As it is taught:

1. **Where any death is concerned he severs the stiff border only for his father and mother, as in the view of R. Meir.**

2. **R. Judah says: Any tear which does not sever the stiff border is a random tear.**

H.   So what is the outcome? The ruling for the High Priest is more strict[20] insofar as he must sever the stiff border.

The passage displays the disjunctive redactional character so typical of the Yerushalmi. Nevertheless, we can identify a fairly smooth flow of discussion in the sequence of A-B+D+F-G+H, moving cogently from the Yohanan/Leazar dispute, through the Meir/Judah citation, on to the resolution at H. The interpolation of the narrative at C has caused problems. Irrelevant to the issue at A-B, it requires the clumsy intervention of E to establish some sort of relationship with the rest of the discussion.

The real problem, however, is not the redaction of the pericope, but its failure to address the matter staked out at A-B. Yohanan and Leazar want to know where the High Priest tears his garment, while the subsequent discussion, until H, deals with the question of when the ritual is obligatory. As a whole, then, the Yerushalmi's entire treatment of A-B is flawed by a failure to clearly identify the issues under dispute and to explain how the evidence of G relates to them.

By way of contrast, observe the clarity of the Bavli's discussion of its own version of A-B:

D'.   They retorted:

1. **Where any death whatever is concerned—if he wants to, he can sever the stiff border; if he wants to, he need not sever the stiff border.**

2. **Upon [the death of] his father or mother he must sever it.**

---

[20]HWMR: following the reading of Y. M.Q. 83d/Y. San. 20a, in accord with the textual apparatus of ed. Romm. See also G. Wewers, *Uebersetzung der Talmud Yerushalmi: Band IV/8. Horayot. Entscheidigung* (Tuebingen: 1984), p. 95, n. 258.

E'. Since [complete severing] is the normal sense of "tear", apply here the verse: NOR REND HIS GARMENTS (Lev. 21:10) [which proves that the report at D', which applies to commoners, has no bearing upon the practice of the High Priest]!

F'. Samuel holds the view of R. Judah, who said: **Any tear which does not sever the edge is nothing but a random tear.**

G'. What then? [If you claim that Samuel holds the view of R. Judah,] does R. Judah require rending in the case of the High Priest [as does Samuel]?

Yet indeed it is stated in a Tannaitic source:

...Scripture states: **HE SHALL NEITHER LET HIS HAIR GROW NOR REND HIS GARMENTS. Thus the commandments of letting the hair grow wild and rending the garments have absolutely no bearing upon him [i.e., the High Priest]—the words of R. Judah....** (Sifra Emor, par. 2:3)

H'. Samuel holds the view of R. Judah on one point [that commoners must totally sever their garment], and takes issue with him on one point [concerning the High Priest's obligation to make a tear].

Like the Palestinian discussion, the Bavli's seeks the basis of the views behind its introductory dispute. Similarly, the Bavli adduces as evidence an unattested Tannaitic source (D'+F' = Yerushalmi G). Beyond this, however, the two discussions have little in common.

Unlike the Yerushalmi's unit, the composite character of which created a number of problems, the Bavli's develops in close pursuit of its original concern—to explain both the nature of the High Priest's mourning rite and the views upon it held by the principal protagonists of the unit. While the Bavli clearly knows materials known also to the editor of the Palestinian unit, it is unaware of the difficulties which clumsy redaction has introduced into the latter, and shows no inclination to resolve these by recasting the Palestinian material more successfully. The Bavli, in fact, fails altogether to engage the complexities raised by the Yerushalmi. The latter, therefore, in its extant form, is not a source for the Babylonian redactor; rather, Palestinian sources—an Amoraic dispute about M. 3:6 and a Tannaitic tradition about ritual tearing—known to the editor of the Yerushalmi's discussion have likewise found their way into the hands of the Babylonian, who shapes them in accord with his own interests.

This survey of representative textual correspondences has, as predicted, duplicated for the Horayot tractates results already reached by earlier practitioners of tradition-historical criticism of the Talmudic literature as a whole. Despite undeniable textual resonances between the two works, the extant Yerushalmi seems to have played little or no role in the processes by which Palestinian learning and its results were transmitted to Babylonian Amoraim. Rather, insofar as the Babylonians of the fourth and fifth centuries knew their colleagues' traditions, they seem to have known them from sources other than the extant Yerushalmi.

But does this same judgment apply to the sixth century figures responsible for the later compilation of Amoraic materials into tractates of Mishnah commentary? To answer this question we must move from comparison of discrete literary units to a different strategy of comparative study.

Structural Correspondences in the Horayot Tractates

We turn attention now to structural correspondences between the Palestinian and Babylonian commentaries on Mishnah Horayot; that is, similar patterns by which discrete pericopae in each tractate are organized into larger units of exegetical discourse serving the Mishnah. To the extent that such correspondences are demonstrated it is appropriate to consider the possibility that the editorial choices of the Babylonian redactors of a Mishnah commentary reflect decisions already made for them by their Palestinian predecessors.

In order to provide some controls for this analysis, I have divided the two tractates into their gross literary units. This is a necessarily subjective exercise, particularly in the Yerushalmi, where the redactional links are so generally loose. Nevertheless, analysis without such basic textual subdivisions is impossible. In any event, each tractate contains roughly 80-90 discrete units of discussion. Thus, while the Bavli is longer than the Yerushalmi in simple quantity of text, the two tractates are rather comparable in the raw number of exegetical pericopae selected for redaction with the Mishnah.

This constitutes to my mind no evidence whatsoever of the Yerushalmi's influence upon the Bavli. But it does help place in perspective a somewhat more interesting fact. Namely, the two Talmuds agree not only in the gross number of exegetical units supplied to Mishnah Horayot, *but also in the amount of attention they are willing to supply to each Mishnaic pericope.* The following list, which shows the number of units appended by each Talmud to each Mishnaic pericope[21] speaks for itself.

> M. 1:1   Y—11, B—14   M.2:5   Y— 3, B— 1

---

[21]See note 13 for the Mishnaic divisions used here and the above appendix for the actual enumeration of literary units. Note that this enumeration ignores the scribal divisions of the gemara, by which materials are assigned to this or that Mishnaic text. Rather, the catalog lists the number of pericopae actually devoted to a given Mishnaic unit on the basis of the content of discussion.

M. 1:2	Y— 3, B— 3		M. 2:6	Y— 2, B— 3
M. 1:3	Y— 3, B— 4		M. 2:7-8	Y— 3, B— 4
M. 1:4	Y— 2, B— 2		M. 3:1-2	Y— 2, B— 2
M. 1:5	Y— 2, B— 1		M. 3:3	Y—17, B—23
M. 1:6-8	Y— 9, B— 6		M. 3:4	Y— 4, B— 2
M. 2:1	Y— 2, B— 2		M. 3:5	Y— 1, B— 1
M. 2:2	Y— 1, B— 3		M. 3:6	Y— 3, B— 1
M. 2:3	Y— 2, B— 2		M. 3:7	Y— 3, B— 4
M. 2:4	Y— 3, B— 3		M. 3:8	Y— 9, B—10

The first type of evidence, then, that the editors of Bavli Horayot had something like our present Yerushalmi Horayot before them lies in the close correspondence in both tractates of the amount of attention, in terms of distinct exegetical initiatives, deemed appropriate for each Mishnaic unit. Where the Yerushalmi treats the Mishnah at length (e.g., M. 1:1, 3:3, 3:8), so too does the Bavli. When the Yerushalmi deems a given Mishnaic passage worthy of little comment (e.g., M. 1:4-5, 2:1-3, 3:5), we find the same judgment in the Bavli. The Bavli, so to speak, is wholly dependent upon a "rhythm" of exegesis—an ebb and flow of major and minor exegetical elaboration—set forth first in the Yerushalmi's contribution to Mishnah Horayot.

The second sort of evidence to which I appeal also focuses upon the redactional choices made by the Bavli's editors. Of interest are materials of a legal, homiletic or narrative character which, while bearing perhaps a general thematic relevance to the issues addressed in Mishnah Horayot, have no clear literary origin in the interpretation of a given pericope of the Mishnah. To the extent that the Bavli's location of such materials coincides with that of the Yerushalmi, we may suggest that the decisions of the latter had some influence over the redactors of the former. Here there are far fewer materials to discuss. But it remains the case that in 11 of 12 cases, an Amoraic discussion which has no essential exegetical relationship to any Mishnaic passage is redacted in both tractates with the *identical* Mishnaic passage.[22]

---

[22]The 12 units are as follows. Only item two is not synchronized in each Talmud.

1. 45d, 14-15 ('YN-BD')/2a, 10-12 ('MR-TM); cf. ls. 21-23

2. 45d, 64-74 (HPRYŠ-ḤṬTW)/11a, 31-35 (D'MR-HW')

3. 47c, 39-56 (R"ŠBL-'WTW)/11a-b, 57-7 (TNW-LDYDHW)

4. 47c, 35-46 (TNY-LDRWTYKM)/11b, 22-30 (T"R-WMLKYM)

5. 47c, 46-48 ('YN-YŠR'L)/12a, 34-36 (T"R-GYḤWN)

6. 47c, 48-51 ('YN-MŠYḤH)/11b, 35-43 ('MR-YWRM)

7. 47c, 51-52 (WL'-NMŠḤW)/12a, 15 ('MR-DKY')

One example must suffice. In their exegesis of M. 1:1, both tractates make room for a statement of Samuel regarding the kind of judicial error required to excuse the community from responsibility for a pollution offering in atonement for inadvertent transgression of a divine prohibition (cf. Lev. 4:13ff). The Yerushalmi's version is as follows (Y. 45d, ls. 14-15):

A. [They] are obliged [for a communal pollution offering] only when they [i.e., the court] offer instructions which partially nullify and partially sustain [a Scriptural prohibition] (M. 2:2).

B. Samuel said: And this holds [only] if they ruled that an act was permitted [and then the people complied]. But if [after the fact of transgression, the court] ruled that it [i.e., the community] is exempt [from obligation]—this amounts to nothing.

Samuel's point is that the type of judicial error which absolves the community from the need for atonement is one in which the court erroneously instructs the community to commit a transgression, rather than a case of the court's *post facto* ratification of a transgression already committed without prior judicial instructions. Be that as it may, the comment does not relate to M. 1:1, which is concerned only with *individual* transgressions inspired by judicial error. The ruling, framed in fact as a gloss of M. 2:2, finds its place here only because it is part of a larger complex of brief glosses which are thematically appropriate overall to M. 1:1.

Compare now the version of the Bavli (2a):

A. Said Samuel: The court is never obliged [to bring a pollution offering in conjunction with communal atonement] unless it says to them: "You are permitted".

B. R. Dimi of Nehardea said: Unless it says to them: "You are permitted to act".

Samuel's lemma differs in content, formal preservation and redactional context from its Palestinian version, but makes a similar point.[23] Here, Samuel's opinion is framed in language permitting it to circulate in the formal context of

---

8. 47c, 53-55 ('YN-QYYMT)/12a, 42-47 ('MR-MLKWTN)

9. 47c, 55-63 ('YN-THTYW)/11b, 43-49 (W'T-ṢDQYHW)

10. 47c, 63-68 (HMŠWH-HQWDŠ)/12a, 1-13 (WMY-ŠM)

11. 48c, 6-8 (TNY-'MY)/14a, 11-14 ('MR-HLYP)

12. 48c, 41-48 (RBY-HQWDŠ)/13b, 30-55 (T"R-NSY')

[23]For further discussion of the relation between the two traditions ascribed to Samuel, see D. Sperber, "A Sugya in Tractate Horayot" [Hebrew], *Sinai* 70 (1972), pp. 157-158.

a dispute, rather than in the form of a Mishnaic gloss. The Bavli places it as well in an entirely new literary setting, where the dispute itself becomes the subject of further exegetical discourse, including the claim that the two opinions ought to be reversed, with Dimi holding Samuel's view and vice versa.

The larger unit, however, is neither formulated in light of M. 1:1 nor of any help in elucidating it, save for a concluding section which cites the Mishnah in order to support the view ascribed at A to Samuel. The whole, in fact, is far more relevant to M. 1:5-8, where the issue of communal atonement is discussed in detail. It appears, then, that the Yerushalmi's correlation of Samuel's view with M. 1:1, even though perhaps only an after-thought in that context, has provided the Bavli's editors with a model for utilizing their own version of his ruling.

A third and related type of parallel concerns the genres of discourse appended in each tractate to a given Mishnaic passage. The majority of the materials in each tractate are careful legal exegeses of the Mishnah. Where, however, the tractates do supply materials of a homiletical-exegetical or theological character, they do so for identical Mishnaic pericopae and supply materials of strikingly similar thematic content, even where explicit textual relations are not demonstrable.

In both tractates material of homiletic or theological character is clustered around the exegesis of M. 3:3-5 and M. 3:8. We begin with a discussion of the former. There is nothing in particular about the content of the Mishnaic materials which might lead us to predict extensive homiletic treatment by the Talmuds, for the Mishnaic sources are themselves legal in theme. After establishing, first of all, that Scriptural laws of atonement applicable to the Anointed Priest and Ruler govern as well the atonement rites of the Solomonic Priest and the Monarch, the Mishnah goes on to specify a series of obligations incumbent upon the Solomonic Priest from which his counterpart in the second Temple is exempt.

As we have already seen, the Talmuds agree in devoting great attention to these Mishnaic rulings, with the Yerushalmi providing 22 units (15 of an aggadic character) and the Bavli 26 (again, with 15 aggadic units). This concentration of the aggadic genre, itself a surprise, is made even more remarkable by the striking character of the thematic correspondences, as the following summary indicates:[24]

---

[24]Omitted from this catalogue are three other items which, because they are either purely legal-exegetical in character or are simply common citations of Tannaitic sources, cannot be used in this context as evidence of thematic correspond. See 47c-d, 68-3/12b, 14-31; 47d, 3-31/12a-b, 51-14; 47d, 56-65/12b. 31-44.

Y. 47a, 1s. 39-56/B.11a-b, 1s. 57-13: Judah the Patriarch enters into conflict with younger Sages over the relation of his office to that of the Mishnah's Ruler.

47c, 21-29/10b, 2-28: Contrastive exegesis of Lev. 4:22 and Qoh. 8:14 leads Yohanan b. Zakkai to link the Ruler's atonement offering with the future life of Israel in the world to come.

47c, 35-46/11b, 22-33: The miraculous qualities of the anointing oil prepared by Moses (Ex. 30:23-31)

47c, 46-48/12a, 34-42: Kings should be anointed near a running stream.

47c, 48-51/11b, 33-55: A history of successionary feuding in the Northern Kingdom.

47c, 51-52/11b, 42-43: The vanished anointing oil is replaced by oil of balsam.

47c, 53-55/12a, 42-47: Y.'s baraita about the superiority of anointing from a horn appears, in B., as part of a Sage's advice to his sons regarding pursuit of Torah in humility.

47c, 55-63/11b, 49-52: Etymological derivations of the names Shallum and Zedekiah.

47c, 63-68/12a, 1-14: T. Sot. 13:1 undergirds two discussions of the Solomonic Temple's superiority over the second Temple.

Clearly, the Talmuds' aggadic supplements to M. 3:3-5 share a common agenda of historical interests in relation to the Mishnah that could not have been remotely predicted from the nature of the Mishnah's discussion itself. Thus the evidence of the Bavli's dependence upon the Yerushalmi is here two-fold: (1) the Bavli's choice of exegetical genre (aggadic supplementation of the Mishnah) corresponds entirely to that of the Yerushalmi; (2) the specific themes laid forth in the Bavli are appropriate to and supplement those chosen by the editors of the Yerushalmi.

The comparative evidence of the Talmuds' responses to M. 3:8 is not nearly so one-sided, but is nevertheless provocative. Here the Mishnah offers perhaps the most frequently-cited ruling in all of M. Horayot:

[I]f a disciple of a Sage was of impaired birth (MMZR) and a High Priest was undisciplined [by apprenticeship in the Torah] ('M H'RS), the disciple of a Sage...precedes the...High Priest.

While both tractates are rich in aggadic supplementation of the Mishnah, and share many thematic and textual correspondences, it is more difficult to show Babylonian dependence upon the Yerushalmi, because both documents (Y. 48b, ls. 38-71/B. 13a-b, ls.39-1) are preoccupied with citing and amplifying an earlier Tannaitic expansion of M. 3:8 (T. Hor. 2:5-13). The most striking thematic correspondence, that is, may simply be due to knowledge of a common source of great relevance to any elucidation of M. 3:8.

But other provocative materials appear as well. We should not be surprised, perhaps, that M. 3:8 might inspire the Talmuds to proclaim the virtues of Torah study and discipleship in a variety of ways. But it is striking that each Talmud should provide a classification of the types of intellectual skills commonly found in students (Y. 48c, ls. 6-8/B. 14a, ls. 11-14). Similarly, both Talmuds offer narratives in which the power and prestige of the Patriarch, based upon his political position, is placed in disparaging relation to that of the Sages, based as it is in learning alone (Y. 48c, ls. 41-48/B. 13b, ls. 30-55). In both cases there are no textual connections whatever uniting the Palestinian and Babylonian materials, so there can be no question of common "traditions" used differently in each document. Rather, a thematic overture, introduced in one textual form in the earlier Talmud, receives its echoing complement in the later at a comparable point in Mishnaic discussion.

The foregoing structural correspondences between the two Horayot tractates are, in my view, undeniable. At issue, of course, is what they mean. Need they suggest that the Babylonian Horayot is in significant measure dependent for its structure upon the Palestinian? Perhaps not, if only a single type of structural correspondence could be discerned. But here we adduce no less than three: (1) quantitative correspondences of materials deemed appropriate to given Mishnaic passages; (2) thematic correspondences in which themes extraneous to a given Mishnaic passage are introduced by both Talmuds at comparable junctures; (3) generic correspondences in which both Talmuds use the same Mishnaic pericopae as opportunities for aggadic supplementation. This appears, then, to constitute grounds for pursuing the possibility that yet other kinds of analyses in the Talmudic literature will yield further evidence of Babylonian reflection upon the Talmud Yerushalmi during the period at which the Babylonian Talmud was taking on its present documentary shape.

Conclusions

The conclusions of this study may be rapidly reviewed. First, the consensus regarding the independence of the Babylonian Talmud from the Palestinian seems in large measure to depend upon a methodological bias toward tradition-historical comparisons between the two literatures. While the comparison of discrete Babylonian Amoraic exegetical units with the extant Yerushalmi does demonstrate a general ignorance of the latter in Babylonia, comparison of larger redactional patterns in document construction yields a rather different picture. The correspondences between Bavli and Yerushalmi Horayot suggest that the post-Amoraic editors of the former had something much like the extant version of the latter before them and reflected upon the logic of its construction as they composed their own commentary.

This judgment about the Yerushalmi's role in setting a kind of literary precedent consulted in Babylonia may help as well to shed light upon the ubiquitous role in the Bavli of large blocks of aggadic materials unconnected in any literary or exegetical sense to the corresponding Mishnaic passage. As we have seen in the Horayot tractates, it is the Palestinian editors who pioneer the thematic lines of aggadic supplementation which are, in turn, appropriated almost without fail by the Babylonians for further elaboration. Only comparative study of other tractates for which both Talmuds exist will determine the extent to which key decisions regarding the introduction of Amoraic aggadah into the larger context of Mishnaic exegesis were made for the editors of the Bavli by their Palestinian predecessors. In sum—apart from the Bavli's obvious independence in deciding details of law and exegesis—its conception of its task and its overall judgment regarding the proper content of a Mishnah commentary seem far more dependent upon the inspiration of the Land of Israel than historians of the literature have been willing to acknowledge.[25]

APPENDIX
TABLE OF TALMUDIC UNITS ACCORDING TO MISHNAIC SEQUENCE

Mishnah	Yerushalmi		Bavli
1:1	1.	45c, 59-63	2a, 10-31
	2.	45c, 63-75	2a, 32-47
	3.	45c-d, 75-6	2a-b, 47-1
	4.	45d, 6-13	2b, 2-10
	5.	45d, 14-17	2b, 10-21
	6.	45d, 17-20	2b, 22-25
	7.	45d, 20-29	2b-3a, 26-7
	8.	45d, 29-47	3a, 7-32
	9.	45d, 47-51	3a, 33-36

[25]The style and argument of this paper would have been much the poorer without the careful comments of my colleague, Bernard Levenson, Stroum Post-Doctoral Fellow in Jewish Studies at the University of Washington. I wish also to thank Profs. Y. Elman (Yeshiva University), R. Sarason (HUC-JIR) and, especially, the editor of the present volume, for without their encouragement I would never have attempted to wrestle the original paper into presentable form. The usual absolution, of course, applies here as well.

	10.	45d, 52-64	3a, 36-40
	11.	5d, 64-74	3a, 40-46
	12.		3a-b, 46-2
	13.		3b, 2-29
	14.		3b, 30-35
1:2	1.	45d-46a, 74-10	3b, 42-48
	2.	46a, 10-16	3b-4a, 48-13
	3.	46a, 16-22	4a, 14-17
1:3	1.	46a, 23-27	4a, 18-40
	2.	46a, 27-34	4a, 40-43
	3.	46a, 34-43	4a, 43-53
	4.		4b, 1-26
1:4	1.	46a, 44-48	4b, 33-39
	2.	46a, 48-52	4b, 39-42
1:5	1.	46a, 52-55	4b, 43-46
	2.	46a, 55-60	
1:6-8	1.	46a, 61-72	5a-b, 17-13
	2.	46a-b, 72-6	5b, 13-34
	3.	46b, 7-14	5b, 34-40
	4.	46b, 15-23	5b, 40-46
	5.	46b, 23-38	5b-6a, 46-40
	6.	46b, 28-34	6a-b, 40-30
	7.	46b, 34-38	
	8.	46b, 38-46	
	9.	46b, 46-56	
2:1	1.	46c, 15-28	6b, 34-40
	2.	46c, 28-31	6b-7a, 40-33
2:2	1.	46c, 31-41	7a-b, 39-1
	2.		7b, 1-20
	3.		7b, 20-31
2:3	1.	46c, 41-47	7b, 35-42
	2.	46c, 47-52	7b-8a, 42-13
2:4	1.	46c, 53-60	8a, 17-37
	2.	46c, 60-73	8a, 37-45
	3.	46c-d, 73-8	8a-b, 35-6

2:5	1.	46d, 8-14	8b, 13-34
	2.	46d, 14-31	
	3.	46d, 31-36	
2:6	1.	46d, 36-43	8b-9a, 40-9
	2.	46d, 43-47	9a, 9-12
	3.		9a, 12-31
2:7-8	1.	46d, 49-55	9a-b, 46-5
	2.	46d, 55-65	9b, 5-14
	3.	46d, 65-73	9b, 15-26
	4.		9b, 26-32
3:1-2	1.	47a, 32-39	9b-10a, 39-5
	2.	47a, 39-56	10a, 5-17
3:3	1.	47a, 56-69	10a, 22-36
	2.	47a-b, 69-1	10a, 36-43
	3.	47b, 1-21	10a-b, 43-2
	4.	47b, 21-30	10b, 2-11
	5.	47b, 31-59	10b, 11-28
	6.	47b, 59-63	10b, 28-40
	7.	47b-c, 63-10	10b, 40-44
	8.	47c, 10-21	10b, 44-50
	9.	47c, 21-29	10b, 50-53
	10.	47c, 29-33	10b-11a, 53-7
	11.	47c, 33-35	11a, 7-24
	12.	47c, 35-46	11a, 24-43
	13.	47c, 46-48	11a, 43-49
	14.	47c, 48-52	11a, 49-57
	15.	47c, 53-55	11a-b, 57-13
	16.	47c, 55-63	11b, 22-33
	17.	47c, 63-68	11b, 33-49
	18.		11b, 49-52
	19.		12a, 1-15
	20.		12a, 15-28
	21.		12a, 29-34
	22.		12a, 34-47
	23.		12a, 47-51
3:4	1.	47c-d, 68-3	12a-b, 51-14
	2.	47d, 3-5	12b, 14-31
	3.	47d, 5-31	

	4.	47d, 31-56	
3:5	1.	47d, 56-65	12b, 31-44
3:6	1.	47d, 66-75	12b, 46-53
	2.	47d-48a, 75-13	
	3.	48a, 13-25	
3:7	1.	48a, 25-40	12b, 55-57
	2.	48a, 40-44	12b, 57-58
	3.	48a, 44-69	13a, 1-9
	4.		13a, 9-23
3:8	1.	48a-b, 70-12	13a, 24-36
	2.	48b, 12-19	13a, 39-43
	3.	48b, 19-27	13a, 43-44
	4.	48b, 28-37	13a, 44-46
	5.	48b, 37-71	13a-b, 46-1
	6.	48b-c, 71-6	13b, 2-29
	7.	48c, 6-38	13b, 29-55
	8.	48c, 38-48	13b-14a, 55-11
	9.	48c, 48-61	14a, 11-14
	10.		14a, 14-17

Chapter Two
The Stam and the Final Generations of Amoraim: Assessing the Importance of Their Relationship for Study of the Redaction of the Talmud

Richard Kalmin
The Jewish Theological Seminary

One of the most important issues facing modern Talmudic scholarship is the precise nature of the anonymous, editorial layer of the Talmud, the stam.[1] Full understanding of Talmudic sources is impossible without insight into the role played by the anonymous editors in shaping the final form of these sources. Additions by the stam can take innumerable forms. To describe just a few, statements by Amoraim (Talmudic sages who flourished between the redaction of the Mishnah in about 200 C.E. and the conclusion of the Amoraic period at the beginning of the sixth century C.E.)[2] can be prefaced by an anonymous discussion such that the Amoraim appear to come in response to the anonymous discussion. Or a dialogue between two Amoraim can be resumed by the stam, creating the impression that the Amoraim are continuing to speak. Or material can be interpolated into an Amora's statement, either before, after, or in the middle.

---

[1]See, for example, Hyman Klein, "Gemara and Sebara," *JQR* 38 (1947), pp. 67-91; "Gemara Quotations in Sebara," *JQR* 43 (1953), pp. 341-63; "Some General Results of the Separation of Gemara from Sebara in the Babylonian Talmud," *JSS* 3 (1958), pp. 363-72; David Halivni, *Mekorot u-Mesorot: Yoma-Hagigah, Shabbat, and Eruvin-Pesahim* (Jerusalem: Jewish Theological Seminary, 1975-82); Shamma Friedman, "Al Derekh Heker ha-Sugya," in *Perek ha-Isha Rabbah ba-Bavli* (Jerusalem: Jewish Theological Seminary, 1978); and Richard Kalmin, *The Redaction of the Babylonian Talmud: Amoraic or Saboraic?* (Cincinnati: Hebrew Union College Press, 1988).

[2]The dates mentioned here are based on *Seder Tannaim ve-Amoraim*, ed. Kalman Kahan (Frankfurt am Main: Hermon, 1935), and *Igeret Rav Sherira Gaon*, ed. Benjamin Lewin (Haifa, 1921). The dates provided by these and other post-Talmudic sources for the deaths of Talmudic rabbis are impossible to verify in their exact details. However, it is possible in most instances to compare the gaonic chronology with that reflected by the internal evidence of the Talmud, and to arrive at reliable conclusions regarding the proper sequence of these rabbis and their relationship to one another. We have used the traditional dates, while remaining cognizant of their limitations.

29

Although several of the methods utilized by modern scholars to separate the stam from the original core of the sugya were known already to medieval commentators on the Talmud,[3] it has been primarily over the past several decades that these methods have been developed, refined, and applied systematically. As a result of this systematic application of critical methods, many conclusions by earlier scholars who utilized the Talmud as source material have to be re-evaluated, since at least part of what they assumed to have been said by a particular sage at a particular time is in actuality a later addition to his statement. One important contribution of modern Talmudic scholarship, therefore, has been to enable future treatments of ancient rabbinic sources to base their conclusions more reliably on what the Amoraim actually said.

A second contribution of modern Talmudic scholarship has been to enable the relationship between the stam and the attributed sections of the Talmud to be described with a far greater degree of sophistication. Insight into this relationship is indispensable for understanding the Talmud's redactional process, since the stam is responsible for analyzing, explicating, and, when necessary, emending and completing the Amoraic and Tannaitic strata of the Talmud. Unfortunately, however, modern scholarly attempts at understanding the importance of this relationship for study of the Talmud's redaction have been largely unsuccessful.[4] In the present paper, I would like to illustrate this point by focusing on the relationship between the stam and the Amoraim, and examining the most recent attempt at describing the nature of that relationship in order to draw conclusions regarding the redaction of the Talmud.

One of the most striking features of this relationship is the stam's marked tendency to exhibit signs of chronological discontinuity in its commentary on Amoraic sources. On numerous occasions, analysis of the role played by the anonymous redactors suggests that they are operating at a substantial chronological remove from the Amoraic sources at their disposal. Perhaps my meaning will be clearer if I describe in detail two cases in which the activity of the editors is indicative of chronological distance between the Amoraim and the stam. On B. B.M. 104b, we learn that it was the custom in certain localities to record double the amount of the actual dowry in the marriage contract in order to make the sums involved in the contract appear more impressive than they actually were. We find that a very late Amora by the name of Maremar, however, used to allow the husband to collect the full amount written into the marriage contract even when the actual value had been doubled. Ravina objects against Maremar, in Maremar's presence, on the basis of an earlier source that

---

[3]See Shamma Friedman, op. cit., pp. 12ff.

[4]See Richard Kalmin, op. cit., chapters 1 and 7.

states explicitly that when the dowry has been doubled, only half, that is, the actual value, is collected. The sugya concludes with the response to Ravina: "There is no difficulty. This (Maremar's collection of the full amount) is a case where possession was formally effected, while this (the ruling of the earlier source) is a case where possession was not formally effected."

As the sugya is presently structured, we would expect this concluding response to be Maremar's rejoinder to Ravina, since Ravina has just objected against Maremar, in Maremar's presence, and we are given no indication of a change of speaker. It is unlikely, however, that Maremar, in referring to his own action, would say, "This is a case where...." More likely, he would have said, "In the case I was involved in....," or something to that effect. The phraseology presently employed indicates that a third party, the stam, has intervened, and is referring to Maremar's action.

Why did Maremar not make his own reply, leaving it instead to the stam to reply on his behalf? Most likely, Maremar originally did answer Ravina's objection, but his answer has not been preserved. The stam thus did not receive the full text of the dialogue between Maremar and Ravina, two of the latest Amoraim mentioned in the Talmud, and had to supply the missing response. The corrupt state in which this Amoraic dialogue reached the stam in this context is easily explicable if we posit a gap of chronology between the late Amoraim who comprise the core of the discussion and the anonymous editors who add to their discussion.

A second passage which indicates chronological distance between the stam and the late Amoraim is found on B. A.Z. 62b-63a. In this discussion, we read that the house of R. Yannai borrowed fruit that grew during the Sabbatical year and returned the monetary equivalent of the fruit in the eighth year, that is, the year following the Sabbatical year. They borrowed the fruit while it was still permitted, and paid their debt after the fruit would have become forbidden. In the meantime, however, the borrowed fruit had been totally consumed, and was not in existence when the prohibition of the Sabbatical year took effect.

Against this practice of the house of R. Yannai, Rav Sheshet objects, on the basis of a Baraita which states that it is forbidden for an employer to instruct his laborers to buy food and drink as payment for their wages, with the promise that he, the employer, will pay their grocery bill. The worry is that the laborers, if they are non-Jews, or Jews who are not scrupulous about tithing, will buy forbidden food and drink. When the employer pays their bill, his money turns out to be in exchange for forbidden goods. Similarly, the money used by the house of R. Yannai to pay their debt was in exchange for now-forbidden fruit, and should therefore also be forbidden.

As several medieval commentators point out, however, Rav Sheshet's objection against the house of R. Yannai is difficult. R. Shlomo ben Adret gives perhaps the clearest and most succinct account of this difficulty, pointing out that in the Baraita quoted by Rav Sheshet, the laborers are actually eating forbidden food and drinking forbidden wine, so when the Jew pays the storekeeper for what the laborer eats, he is paying for forbidden goods. In the case of the house of R. Yannai, however, at the time the produce was borrowed it was still permitted, and when the prohibition took effect the produce had already been consumed. When the monetary equivalent was returned, therefore, the money was not in exchange for forbidden goods.

It therefore seems likely that the discussion beginning with Rav Sheshet on 62b and concluding with the dialogue between Rav Yemar and Rav Ashi on 63a was not originally based on the case involving the house of R. Yannai. This discussion appears to have originally been based on Rav Yehuda's quotation of Rav on B. A.Z. 71a. Rav says there, "A man is permitted to say to an idolater: 'Go and settle for me the king's portion.'" Rav Sheshet interpreted the phrase "the king's portion" in Rav's statement to refer to food and drink, and asks: How can Rav say that a Jew is allowed to tell an idolater to give on his behalf the share of food that is due from him to the king, and need not worry that the idolater will pay his share with forbidden food and drink? In the words of R. Yom-Tov ben Avraham Ishbili: "After all, he [the Jew] must pay the non-Jew the value of the wine that he gave at his [the Jew's] command and as his messenger. It is therefore as if he [the Jew] paid his debt with idolatrous wine."[5] Yet according to the Baraita quoted by Rav Sheshet, we do worry that the store owner will give the workers wine used for idolatry, and the employer will thereby have paid his debt with forbidden wine. The Baraita thus appears to be in direct conflict with Rav. Rav Hisda resolves the contradiction by explaining that the Baraita and Rav are dealing with different cases, and so on until the conclusion of the sugya.

This sugya most likely became detached from its original context on B. A.Z. 71a long after the time of Rav Yemar and Rav Ashi, who presently conclude the discussion on 63a. Whoever removed the sugya from its original connection did not understand Rav as I interpreted him above, and as all the Amoraim from Rav Sheshet through Rav Yemar and Rav Ashi interpret him, but rather as the medieval commentators on 71a interpret him.[6] Rather than permitting a Jew to

---

[5]Ritba on B. A.Z. 71a.

[6]See, for example, Tosafot. We arrive at the same conclusion if we interpret Rav in accordance with Rashi on B. A.Z. 71a. According to Rashi, Rav permits a Jew to tell an idolater to pay his portion only in a case where the non-Jew has the

tell an idolater to give on his behalf the share of food that is due from him to the king, Rav is permitting a Jew to tell an idolater to discharge his debt of food to the king by any means at the idolater's disposal. The Baraita quoted by Rav Sheshet is no longer difficult according to this understanding of Rav, since the Baraita specifies that the employer is instructing his workers to go out and buy food: "Go out and eat and I will pay. Go out and drink and I will pay." Consequently, when the workers go out and buy idolatrous wine, the owner is counted as having illegally discharged his debt.

The stam's interpretation of Rav contrasts with the interpretation of Rav presupposed by all of the Amoraim mentioned on 62b-63a. The stam did not understand the Amoraic comments in their original context, and therefore transferred them to a new context where he felt they were more appropriate.

The two cases described above illustrate that the characteristic forms of anonymous editorial activity vis-a-vis early Amoraic sources, for example transferring Amoraic statements from their original contexts to new locations, or adding to Amoraic discussions, creating the impression that the Amoraim are continuing to speak, are observable in connection with statements by late Amoraim as well. In the two examples analyzed above, the anonymous editors appeared to be operating at a substantial chronological remove from some of the latest Amoraim mentioned in the Talmud. The question is, however, whether or not these cases are typical of the stam's treatment of late Amoraic sources. If they are typical, then we would be justified in positing an extremely late date for at least substantial portions of the Talmud's anonymous, editorial commentary. If they are atypical, then can any conclusions be drawn regarding the date of the composition of the stam?

This writer's examination of the stam based on the statements by late Amoraim reveals that signs of chronological distance between the stam and the late Amoraim are rare. The number of cases in which the stam misunderstands statements by a late Amora is quite small. In addition, it is rare for the stam and the late Amoraim to be working with opposing versions of the same sources. For example, when we can determine which version of a Tannaitic source a late Amoraic statement is based on, it is rare to find the stam based upon an opposing version of the same source. The stam and the late Amoraim thus had before them the same basic corpus of material. Finally, it is rare for the stam

---

option of providing the monetary equivalent of the portion owed by the Jew. Therefore, the Baraita quoted by Rav Sheshet, which specifies that a Jew directs his non-Jewish laborers to eat and drink, no longer poses a difficulty for Rav.

not to have received the full text of statements by late Amoraim, or not to have received the original context of their statements.[7]

David Halivni claims that the paucity of evidence for the existence of chronological distance between the stam and the Amoraim living after the death of Rav Ashi (in approximately 427 C.E.[8]) is in stark contrast to what we find in connection with the stam based on all previous Amoraic generations. Halivni argues that this stark contrast helps prove his contention that anonymous redaction began following the death of Rav Ashi and ended with the death of the last Amora early in the sixth century C.E. He maintains that the contemporaneity between the redactors and the Amoraim who lived during this period accounts for the (supposed) atypical relationship between them.[9]

Upon closer examination, however, this argument in favor of dating the anonymous redaction of the Talmud to the approximately one hundred years following the death of Rav Ashi turns out to be inadequate. In the first place, examination of the stam commentary on Rav Ashi's contemporaries reveals only minor variations between this layer of stam and the stam based on even the latest Amoraim mentioned in the Talmud.[10] Perhaps more importantly, at present we lack the criteria necessary for calculating in any precise fashion how chronological distance between redactor and source determines the level of discontinuity between them. We cannot say with any degree of reliability, for example, how much evidence of chronological distance we would expect to find in an anonymous discussion separated by 50, 100, or 200 years from its sources. Such precision, if it is attainable at all, will have to wait until we have a full picture of the stam based on every Amoraic generation.

When we turn to a second characteristic feature of stam commentary, its sheer volume and its tendency towards complexity and prolixity, our results reveal much about the behavior of the stam. But once again, they do not allow us to conclude anything about the date of the its composition. We find that the stam based on statements by the latest Amoraim is for the most part extremely simple

---

[7]See Richard Kalmin, op. cit., chapter 7, and Richard Kalmin, *The Post-Rav Ashi Amoraim: Transition or Continuity? A Study of the Role of the Final Generations of Amoraim in the Redaction of the Talmud* (Ann Arbor: University Microfilms International, 1985), pp. 288-366.

[8]See *Seder Tannaim ve-Amoraim*, p. 5, and *Igeret Rav Sherira Gaon*, p. 94. See also note 2, above.

[9]David Halivni, *Midrash, Mishnah, and Gemara; The Jewish Predilection for Justified Law* (Cambridge, Massachusetts: Harvard University Press, 1986), pp. 83-4, and 142-43, note 19.

[10]See Richard Kalmin, *The Redaction of the Babylonian Talmud: Amoraic or Saboraic?*, chapter 7.

and brief, in marked contrast to stam commentary in general. We never find the stam making statements by the latest Amoraim the basis for sugyot of any degree of complexity. Most typically, the stam based on statements by the latest Amoraim consists of no more than a simple objection and response, or a brief halachic decision, and the like.

Analysis of the anonymous commentary on contemporaries of Rav Ashi, however, reveals that these features of brevity and simplicity, uncharacteristic as they are of stam commentary in general, are not unique to the stam based on the latest Amoraim. We find that the stam, in its commentary on statements by contemporaries of Rav Ashi, exhibits these same characteristics to almost exactly the same degree.[11]

We can account for the thin layer of anonymous commentary on late Amoraim by pointing out that the anonymous editors were concerned with raising and resolving difficulties, filling in lacunae, and the like, in the Amoraic and Tannaitic material that had been transmitted to them. Since these editors were relatively near in time to the latest Amoraic generations, and they therefore received the statements by these Amoraim basically intact, there was relatively little that required their editorial concern.

In addition, in order to account for the fact that there is virtually no difference between the level of stam based on contemporaries of Rav Ashi and that based on the latest Amoraim mentioned in the Talmud, we can posit that the stam made a conscious decision to comment extensively on traditions that had chronological priority, and to ignore later traditions almost entirely. The stam commented on Tannaitic and early Amoraic statements to the virtual exclusion of the late Amoraic sections of the Talmud.

The claim that chronological priority played an important role in the editing of the Talmud is not mere conjecture on my part, for we encounter a related phenomenon in the tendency of the stam to concentrate its commentary on the beginnings of individual chapters, and on the beginning of tractates, far more than on later chapters.[12] That is, here as well we see that the stam comments more or less on certain passages based on its conception of what was or was not an appropriate subject of commentary. Priority, both in terms of chronology and location within a tractate, was one factor determining for the stam what most immediately required its attention.

---

[11] Richard Kalmin, ibid.

[12] See Shamma Friedman, op. cit., pp. 48-49.

Chapter Three
The Beginings of the Preservation of Argumentation in Amoraic Babylonia

David C. Kraemer
Jewish Theological Seminary

The agenda defined by the Mishnah is to a significant extent the subject of the Gemara's deliberations as well.[1] But the manner in which their common agenda is addressed is radically different, and this difference is perhaps most evident at the first level of approach to these respective texts, that is, in their dissimilar styles of presentation. The Mishnah presents simple opinions or differences of opinion. It does not record the deliberations that produced these opinions. The Gemara, on the other hand, chose to express itself primarily through the deliberations that produced the final opinions. In order, then, to understand the development of the Gemara as a literary text, and before we can consider the motivations of its authors, it is essential to ask when these deliberations joined the conclusions as objects of preservation.

Of course, this question has been asked before.[2] But finding a solution has been complicated by a variety of difficulties. First, the anonymous Gemara text, that segment of the text that is most replete with the deliberations whose source of preservation we seek, is of unknown origin. The chronology of the anonymous sections is at least in doubt, and according to recent consensus they

---

[1]But see Jacob Neusner, *Judaism: The Classical Statement* (Chicago, 1986), pp. 94-114 and 222-240. I have taken issue with Neusner's precise conclusions in my "Scripture Commentary in the Bavli: A Primary or Secondary Phenomenon," in *AJS Review*, March, 1989, forthcoming. Of course, the broad approaches of these two documents are so clearly distinct as to reflect different overall agendas. For a lengthy discussion of the significance of these differences see D. Halivni, *Midrash, Mishnah and Gemara: The Jewish Predeliction for Justified Law* (Cambridge and London, 1986), pp. 38-92.

[2]R. Sherira Gaon (10th cent.) in his famous epistle already offers one suggestion concerning the beginning of the preservation of deliberations in the Gemara; see ed. Levin, pp. 62-64. Most modern scholars of Rabbinic literature have also proposed solutions to this question, generally by seeking the "antiquity of the sugya." See, e.g., A. Weiss, *On the Literary Production of the Amoraim* (Hebrew) (New York, 1961), p. 7ff.; H. Albeck, *Introduction to the Talmuds* (Hebrew) (Tel Aviv, 1969), pp. 576-596; B. DeVries, *Studies in Talmudic Literature* (Hebrew) (Jerusalem, 1968), pp. 181-199.

are post-Amoraic.[3] This material is unlikely, therefore, to yield useful information concerning the origins of the preservation of argumentation. Attributed Amoraic material is no more generous in providing evidence that bears on our question. The vast majority of Amoraic deliberations are extremely brief, and the introductory formula "Rabbi X said to Rabbi Y" reveals little concerning their origin. Technical indications of dialogue are so fluid in the manuscripts and versions as to call into question the preservational status of such texts. Unfortunately, the literature was not sufficiently self-conscious to address the process of the formulation of these traditions. As a consequence of this general condition, scholarly conclusions have depended upon subjective analyses of evidence that admittedly yields a variety of interpretations.

I would like to suggest, however, that a crucial body of evidence has been ignored, and that the road to discovering the origin of the preservation of argumentation is not as cluttered as it might appear. What has been overlooked is the fact that when the Amoraic sages acted to preserve their traditions they did, on a good number of occasions, admit to this fact. This, if anything, is the intent of the formula "Rabbi X said Rabbi Y said." The first name in such a couplet, "Rabbi X," reveals to us the name of the authority who repeated a tradition as its primary Tanna. The Tanna, it has been noted,[4] served a function similar to a published book; that is, he assured that the published subject would be preserved. When Amoraim act in this position, then, they are stating their commitment to the preservation of such traditions. Moreover, these formulas reveal that it was not only anonymous academic functionaries who acted in this fashion, but some of the most prominent sages of the Amoraic era.[5] Even were we to consider the possibility that such chains of tradition are sometimes artificial constructs, we would still be forced to admit that such attributions serve

---

[3]See a review of the relevant literature in D. Goodblatt, "The Babylonian Talmud," in J. Neusner, ed., *The Study of Ancient Judaism. Vol. II* (Ktav Publishing, 1981), pp. 154-7 and 177-181. See also Richard Kalmin's paper in this volume.

[4]See S. Lieberman, "The Publication of the Mishnah," in *Hellenism in Jewish Palestine* (New York, 1950), pp. 83-99. Lieberman astutely points out that the question is not whether Rabbinic traditions were ever written, but whether authoritative versions took a written form or not. He concludes that they did not, and I remain convinced that published authoritative traditions were preserved orally. See also J. Neusner, *The Pharisees: Rabbinic Perspectives* (New Jersey, 1973), pp. 225-27, and "Tannaim," in *The Encyclopedia of Religion* (New York, 1987), vol. 14, p. 272.

[5]Note especially the activity of R. Judah in this regard. See B. Kosowsky, *Otsar Hashemot Latalmud Bavli*, (Jerusalem, 1977), vol. 2, pp. 637-54.

to enhance the position of the Tanna. In doing so they also assure that traditions whose survival is dependent upon this process will be preserved. But at the same time it is crucial to note that the form of traditions that the Amoraim admit to preserving is limited. What is restricted from this process, apparently, is Amoraic argumentation. While any student could point to dozens of examples of Amoraic preservation of brief, categorical traditions, even the most seasoned scholar would be hard-pressed to quote an example of explicit Amoraic preservation of argumentation. Not that such cases do not exist—they do. It is these few rare cases, where Amoraim actually quote Amoraic argumentation, that are most instructive with respect to our question of the origins of the preservation of argumentation.

In a review of the entire Babylonian Talmud, I have discovered only thirty-three cases[6] of explicit preservation of argumentation from the first four Amoraic generations. By "explicit preservation" I mean traditions that approximate the model referred to above, that is, "Rabbi X said Rabbi Y objected to Rabbi Z." Both the chronology of these cases and the precise model of argumentation that was preserved in this way reveal a great deal concerning the beginning of the Babylonian Gemara style.

There are no cases of explicit preservation of argumentation from the first two Amoraic generations.[7] This supports the general observation that stylistically these generations quite closely followed the model established by the Mishnah.[8] The first cases occur in the third generation, and they represent a rather modest beginning.

Third generation sages who explicitly quote earlier argumentation are Zeira,[9] Joseph[10] and Rabba.[11] The traditions quoted are generally brief questions, and they are typified by the direct participation in the earlier argumentation of the individual now quoting it.[12] This suggests that the earliest motivation to repeat

---

[6]This was the number that I discovered in my dissertation research. Since that time a few more have come to my attention. They do not change the analysis that I suggest below.

[7]I have followed the generational divisions proposed by Albeck, op. cit., pp. 144ff.

[8]See I. Halevy, *Dorot Harishonim*, part II, p. 591; A. Weiss, op. cit., pp. 10-11; and David Kraemer, *Stylistic Characteristics of Amoraic Literature* , (Ph.D. diss., Jewish Theological Seminary, 1984; hereafter reffered to as *SCAL*), pp. 47-79.

[9]B. Ber. 48a, B. Men. 7a.

[10]B. Ber. 25b, B. Hul. 36b.

[11]B. Eruv. 17a, 40a and 40b; B. Suk. 17a-b.

[12]See e.g. B. Ber. 25b, 48a and B. Eruv. 17a.

argumentation was a kind of self-consciousness, a thesis that can be supported from other contemporary factors.[13] There are exceptional cases of longer preservation,[14] but these too are characterized by direct personal involvement. The only near-exception to this rule is the preservation by Joseph at B. Hul. 36b, where after beginning with his own involvement, Joseph goes on to quote several steps in which he himself was not directly involved. Still, the beginning of this exchange, and therefore the general motivation, conforms to the previously noted rule.

There are relatively many cases of explicit preservation by sages who are contemporary with the third and fourth generations. Without exception these sages are individuals who served also as messengers of traditions between Palestine and Babylonia. This factor, I will suggest, is central to their position as preservers of argumentation, and not merely coincidental. These cases deserve more lengthy attention, and I will deal with them, therefore, after a brief description of explicit preservation in the fourth generation.

Fourth generation sages are no more prolific in quoting argumentation than their predecessors. While Abbaye quotes one deliberation in which he himself was involved (B. Eruv. 45b), he also sees fit to quote the argumentation of others (B. Eruv. 12a and B. B.M. 10a). Rava preserves argumentation on four occasions, though in two[15] the preserved deliberation is in a less typical narrative form. In one of his other two cases (B. B.M. 10a) Rava is joined by Abbaye in the preservation of argumentation, and this example is particularly significant because the preserved traditions have been transported from Palestine, and because they are very finely formulated. This phenomenon finds numerous parallels, and it leads us now to consider the factor of transport.

In sixteen of the total of thirty-three cases of explicit preservation of argumentation, the preserved argumentation has been transported between Palestine and Babylonia (in either direction, though usually the tradition has originated in Palestine). Six of these traditions are introduced with the formula "when Rabbi X came (from Palestine) he said..." When compared to the traditions preserved within Babylonia, these cases are often far more elaborate, and many exhibit fine literary formulation and reworking. Reference to a few select examples will help to illustrate.

At B. Yeb. 11b-12a R. Hiyya b. Abba repeats an exchange of four steps between R. Johanan and R. Ammi. The deliberation is initiated by R. Johanan's question, and what follows is simple dialogue. What is significant in this case

---

[13]See *SCAL*, pp. 81ff.

[14]See Rabba at B. Eruv. 40b and particularly at B. Suk. 17a-b.

[15]B. Pes. 103a, B. B.M. 48b.

is that R. Nachman b. Isaac, a Babylonian sage (the others are Palestinian), offers an alternative version of the deliberation, which is introduced with the formula "R. Nachman b. Isaac taught it this way (*mtny hky*)." This formula is indicative of a formally constructed tradition, and it means that an exchange whose latest participant was a third generation Palestinian has already assumed a formal literary character in fourth generation Babylonia. It also means that R. Nachman knew Hiyya b. Abba's quotation as a formal preservation. Nor is this a one-time event. Precisely the same phenomenon, relating to a different subject but repeating the structure and participants of this case exactly, is found at B. Zeb. 85b. In neither of these examples does the fact that the tradition was transported to Babylonia from Palestine appear to be central. But equivalent examples of formulation and reformulation of quoted argumentation do not recur in traditions restricted to Babylonia. That fact, when considered in conjunction with related evidence, is certainly significant.

A second example, at B. Hul. 134a-b, is introduced with the "when R. X came from Palestine" formula, in this case R. Dimi being the one who preserves earlier argumentation. The deliberation that originated in Palestine, an exchange between R. Johanan and R. Laqish, is only three steps in length, but the initial step involves a question concerning two contradictory Tannaitic sources, and the steps that follow are also not simple. It is clear that the present formulation is the one repeated by R. Dimi; Rava and Abbaye, both later contemporaries, address it directly. This is significant in that the parallel Palestinian traditions[16] do not retain the dialogical character present here; they are stated as typical categorical Amoraic traditions. We must assume, therefore, that either R. Dimi preserved an exchange that the Palestinians themselves did not see fit to preserve, or that R. Dimi, for some reason, chose to formulate these traditions in a dialogical form. In either case, what stands out is the fact that when transported from Palestine to Babylonia, Dimi quotes not independent traditions, but traditions that relate to one another in argumentational dialogue. Again, a similar phenomenon, with equal elaboration, is not present in exclusively Babylonian traditions.

A third example, at B. Hul. 57a-b, is in certain ways less significant than the previous two. It is, first, a case of explicit preservation in which the individual who repeats the argumentation is personally involved. This is apparently the least sophisticated model of such preservation, as witnessed previously. Second, the whole matter here is not formulated with the same literary exactness as the previous examples. It is part of a longer narrative, and as is the case with

---

[16]See Y. Hal. 3:4 (59b), and Y. Peah ch. 4 end (18c). For a fuller discussion of this example, see *SCAL*, pp. 162ff.

Talmudic narrative in general, it is difficult to evaluate the conditions and chronology of its formulation. On the other hand, the argumentation is repeated quite explicitly on account of transport, in this case from Babylonia to Palestine, and the quoted exchange is far longer than anything we have seen previously, extending to a full eight steps.[17] Here it would be impossible to deny that transport of traditions is somehow significant in motivating the preservation of relevant argumentation.[18]

But why should this be the case? Why, when it is transported, does a conclusive tradition need the elaborative argumentation, while, when it remains in the environs of its creation, it does not? One possible answer is suggested by in the gemara itself, at B. Hul. 51a. In this case, a legal decision that originated in Palestine is reported without elaboration before Abbaye. Confused by the tradition, Abbaye pursues to great lengths the individual who brought it from Palestine, and, when he finally hears the full story, he discovers that the original report had been an incorrect representation of the fuller picture. Brief statements or reports are likely to become confused, in other words, precisely because of their brevity. Brief traditions require interpretation, and in the openness to such interpretation confusion is likely to result.[19] Argumentation, on the other hand, provides a context. Deliberation is itself interpretation, and though it may be more difficult to preserve, in the end it assures more accurate repetition.

When simple traditions were repeated in their home context, interpretation was more secure and confusion less likely to arise. But there was apparently some recognition that simple traditions, when transported over a long distance and to a different milieu, were more open to such confusion. On those rare occasions when it was deemed essential to avoid such confusion, something of the original context was also preserved. For this reason, it would appear, preserved argumentation more often accompanies traditions that were transported between the two great centers of Rabbinic learning.[20]

---

[17]On manuscript variants in the quotation segment, and my evaluation that the printed text ought to be depended upon, see *SCAL*, pp. 170-171, n. 29.

[18]Of the other cases of transported argumentational traditions in quotation, five are quite brief (one or two steps). One of these (B. B.B. 27b) repeats a simple question (a semi-apodictic form, see *SCAL*, pp. 312-318) and the response, one (B. Meilah 21b) a brief textual contradiction (*rmi lih*) and the response, and one (B. Nid. 29a) merely a simple objection. The other three such cases are quite long and elaborate. One (B. Men. 7a) is ten steps or longer, and the other two (B. Bes. 38a-b and B. Hul. 19b) are motivated by provocative points of narrative.

[19]See B. Hul. 124a for an excellent—and amusing—example of this phenomenon.

[20]If transport itself was truly the crucial factor, then we would expect the same phenomenon to have occurred in the transport of traditions from Babylonia to

However, if this is the motivation for preserving argumentation, this means that argumentation has not yet attained a status that demands independent attention. It is quoted in the service of other traditions—to provide a context or to suggest a clarifying interpretation. Because its independent worth is as yet dubious, preservation of such traditions is not yet frequent or systematic. The same may be said, of course, of the more simple preservations found in exclusively Babylonian sources. There, the prevalent model of personal involvement suggests that a sage might quote a deliberation in support of a present opinion. The earlier deliberation, though, is not remarked upon for its own sake. This is, of course, not true of the gemara text in general, where attention to argumentation is often central. Both in scope and intent, then, this is a modest beginning.

Concerning the chronology of this preservation, it is noteworthy that the individuals who were responsible for the transport of traditions, Dimi, Ulla and Rabin in particular, were Palestinian sages of the third-fourth generation (that is, students of R. Johanan; earlier contemporaries of Abbaye and Rava). If their repetition of Palestinian traditions in Babylonia motivated the occasional preservation of an argumentational exchange, then this factor may also have acted as a catalyst for the preservation of argumentation by Babylonian sages themselves. The awakening self-awareness in formulating traditions would certainly have provided fertile ground for such a response, and as we noted, this was precisely the period during which the first explicit preservation is found in Babylonia. It appears to me that the coincidence of these factors is more than a matter of chance.

Moreover, another phenomenon that follows immediately upon this period is indicative of a significant change in preservational sensibilities. What I am referring to is two cases, at B. Git. 25a-b and B. B.M. 55b-56a, where Abbaye comments at length about details of earlier argumentation. The form and nature of his comments is extremely revealing.

In the Gittin text, Abbaye's comment is preceded by three stages of argumentational exchange. Abbaye's tradition, referring to this exchange, is this: "Abbaye said: He asks him X and the other answers Y and he then objects X." I have not translated in full because what is stated in three words in the

---

Palestine. The Babylonian Talmud records that this was in fact the case in a number of instances, and the text referred to above from B. Hul. 57a-b is only one such example. The Yerushalmi also ought to record similar evidence. Though I have not made an extensive search of that document, several examples have come to my attention. For a review of these, see *SCAL*, p. 167.

Hebrew (the language of X and Y; the rest of the comment is in Aramaic)[21] would require many words of explanation in an English translation. The original tradition is as brief as I have here represented it. In the Baba Metsia text Abbaye's comment is longer, but the length is required by the difficulty and sophistication of the argumentation that he is referring to and of the insights that he suggests.[22]

What is true of both traditions is this: both are formulated in the typical categorical Amoraic style (spoken of as "apodictic" by Halivni), and both are entirely dependent upon the retention of the earlier argumentation to which they refer. The categorical form means that these are published traditions. To say that they were "published" means that they were intended to be formally preserved for transmission to future generations. But in these particular cases that preservation could not have been independent. As I said, without the referent argumentation, these traditions are entirely incomprehensible. That means that those who published these traditions of Abbaye (and of Rava, who in each of these two cases responds to Abbaye's observation) assumed that the argumentation would also be preserved.

Furthermore, unlike the previous examples, in each of these texts the primary focus and concern of the author of the traditions is clearly the argumentation itself. Particularly in the Baba Metsia case, it is difficult to posit any function other than commentary on argumentation. This was not the case in the examples of explicit preservation, where the deliberation was not clearly the primary focus. This transition is of extraordinary significance. Because these published traditions are primarily concerned with the argumentation itself, we may conclude that the preservation of that argumentation was also a primary intent of the authors. This is the first time that such a phenomenon occurs, and it is the first time, therefore, that a comment in the true spirit of Gemara has been composed.

Abbaye and Rava are Babylonian sages of the fourth generation (early-to-mid-fourth century). They did, therefore, have the opportunity for direct exchange with and considerable influence by the Palestinian messengers of whom we spoke earlier. Is the chronological proximity of these two phenomena—explicit preservation and published, detailed commentary—a mere coincidence, or was

---

[21]The sharp delineation between Hebrew and Aramaic in Amoraic sources, suggested by some contemporary scholars, needs to be considered with caution. Particularly when quoting earlier sources or employing technical terms, Hebrew and Aramaic might be used in the same tradition.

[22]For a more detailed description of these texts, as well as full textual analysis, see *SCAL*, p. 216ff.

there some kind of direct influence of one on the other? Explicit evidence is not, as far as I am aware, available, yet we might suggest a possible relation by reference to a similar, better known phenomenon.

All would agree that commentary follows the initial publication of a text. It would be absurd to publish a commentary unless one were secure in thinking that the text to which it referred would survive. A text must demonstrate its viability before a commentary is to be composed. That was certainly true of earlier Rabbinic materials. The power of the Mishnah motivated its commentary. Simple Amoraic traditions were preserved before later sages could refer back to them. In all cases the viability of preservation comes first.

This is certainly also the reason that there are no early Amoraic comments on Amoraic argumentation; there were no such comments because argumentation was not formally preserved during that period. But in the third generation for the first time, and particularly in connection with texts that had been transported between Palestine and Babylonia, argumentation was preserved in a formal, intended way. The viability of preserving argumentation was now finally established. And it was precisely at this time, therefore, that the first extended comments on argumentation were published.[23]

Of course, when speaking of a tradition as vast as that of the Bavli, a relatively small number of cases such as this does not, on its own, make for convincing conclusions. But is does open a window to inquiry. It now becomes relevant to ask whether other evidence supports these conclusions. Is there some other feature that characterizes the product of these Amoraic generations that would lead us to believe that it was at this point that argumentation was first formally preserved? For example, considerably more argumentation is recorded in the Bavli in the names of sages of these generations than of previous generations. Could this be explained by our proposal that it was now, for the first time, that the value of such traditions was recognized? What is the nature of the many argumentational traditions attributed to these generations? Do they exhibit evidence of intentional, primary formulation? Are they, on the other hand, different from similar traditions in other generations? Do they tell us anything of their preservation at all?

Whatever, in the end, is the answer to these questions, we may still, at this stage, be confident in making the following claims: Formal preservation of argumentation, on at least a very limited scale, began in the third Amoraic

---

[23]The comments of Abbaye do not refer to argumentation preserved from Palestine. But this does not, I think, effect the viability of what I am proposing. Once the viablity of preserving argumentation was demonstrated, any argumentation became a potential object for such comments.

generation and continued modestly thereafter. The transport of traditions between Palestine and Babylonia played a significant role in this process. Its fruit may be seen in the fourth generation in the first published commentaries on argumentation. These cases are very few in number, and this reflects the fact that attention to argumentation as an independent object of interpretation did not gain complete support in rabbinic circles until several generations later.

What we have discovered in the mid-Amoraic era, then, is merely the seeds of what would later typify Gemara. It may not yet be spoken of as a comprehensive method, but only as a relatively modest proposal; something that would be tested, but not yet widely employed. It was only the authors of the anonymous Gemara who would finally extend the implications of what we have seen here to all of Rabbinic tradition. It was they, in the end, who for the first time understood the functions that argumentation could truly be made to serve.[24]

---

[24]My gratitude is due to the Abbell Fund for its assistance in supporting this project.

Chapter Four

The Character and Construction of a Contrived Sugya: Shevuot 3a-4a

Avram Israel Reisner
Jewish Theological Seminary

As critical study of the Talmud has progressed toward a clearer understanding of the differentiation between the collection of Amoraic materials and the infusions of the anonymous layer of text, we find ourselves uncertain as to the genesis and development of those unattributed segments, particularly where those segments are extensive and independent of the surrounding Amoraic framework.[1] These sections are not made up of definable dicta, as are most of the Amoraic materials. Therefore they do not appear to have been created by the same process of accretion of memorized comments, generation after generation, which we see in the Amoraic materials. Traditionally, it has been assumed that the text of the Talmud was a digest of academic discussions with the running give and take representing if not a full transcript of academic sessions, at least a generalized one. This description took the question and answer format as a true representative of the genesis of the material. The model, then, was of the Tannaitic and Amoraic stories in which more or less natural give and take is reported. When a certain artificiality was noted in some of those question and answer sets, this was readily attributed to the Talmudic style of exaggerated diligence in questioning.

Of late I sense a new version of that picture of the formation of anonymous materials, albeit a much more careful and skeptical one. I refer to the recent writings of my teacher Professor David Halivni, who suggests that in the Amoraic period a conscious choice was made to limit transmission to final dicta and leave the background discussions formally unreported. By contrast, in the period of the stam—the anonymous overlay of the later period—a similarly conscious decision was taken to preserve these background discussions.[2]

[1]This paper was delivered to the Annual Conference of the Society of Biblical Literature/American Academy of Religion at Anaheim, Calif. on Nov. 24, 1985. It relates to material from a dissertation in progress at the Jewish Theological Seminary of America on "The Development and Redaction of Tractate Shevuot, Chapter One," being written under Professor Shamma Y. Friedman.

[2]Professor Halivni presents this position briefly in the introduction to the third volume of his magnum opus, *Sources and Traditions, Tractate Shabbath* (Hebrew)

Implicit in this view is that while the preserved discussions are later than the Amoraic strata, and as such not perfectly reliable as far as their historical accuracy is concerned, nevertheless, they attempt to report what the authors of the stam believed had been, or should have been the generative discussion. This too should produce a picture of "live", multifaceted give and take.

A different model has been proposed, *en passant*, by a number of writers[3]— that the unattributed comments are a second, independent book of commentary on the model of Rashi and Tosafot, that was interwoven with the earlier Amoraic Talmud. This is a cogent model for certain expansions and glosses of the Amoraic texts, but leaves open the question of the nature of the many longer, independently focused unattributed sugyot. Meyer Feldblum, in *PAAJR 37*, finds "three types of anonymous material...1) the completely anonymous sugya, 2) anonymous sugyot which incorporate some Amoraic elements, 3) the essentially Amoraic sugya which contains anonymous interpolations - ranging from brief to extensive explanatory comments." The commentary model, applicable to his third type, is much less useful in describing the first two.

Quite a different model has been proposed by a number of scholars in the previous generation with expressly these longer, more developed unattributed segments in mind—that of the academic lecture.[4]

This model was adumbrated primarily to account for the contributions of the Savoraic period. But it must be noted that the scholars in question knew only a bi-partite division between Amoraic and Savoraic Talmud, and the notion that we are dealing with three segments, Amoraic, stammitic and Savoraic, as opposed to

---

(JTS, 1982), chiefly pp. 9-10. He promises to expand upon it in detail in an English volume, *From the Apodictic to the Discursive: Varieties in the Mode of Classical Jewish Learning* (working title) due to be published soon.

[3]M. Friedmann (Ish Shalom), in a Hebrew monograph entitled *Concerning Talmud: Can It Be Properly Translated* (Vienna, 1885) (referred to by S. Friedman, *Texts and Studies, Analecta Judaica*, Vol. I, pp. 313-314, notes 111, 112), M. Feldblum, "The Impact of the 'Anonymous Sugya' on Halakic Concepts," PAAJR XXXVII, 1960-61, pp. 19-28, D. Halivni, ibid., p. 7, n. 8, and in the introduction to the previous volume, *From Yoma to Hagiga*, pp. 7-8. See, in particular, Dr. Friedman's note 112 for his general discussion of the issues raised in these introductory remarks.

[4]This suggestion is made by N. Brüll, "Die entstellungsgeschichte des Babylonische Talmuds als Schriftwerk," *Jahrbücher für judische Geschichte und Literatur II*, pp. 43-44, and by A. Weiss in his Hebrew monograph *The Opus of the Savoraim*.

simply tending to rename the work of the Savoraim as stam, is far from proven.[5] This latter model proposes that these longer unattributed sections were formed in each instance by a single, disciplined hand in order to make the specific points which constituted the theme of the lecture.

In this paper I propose to dissect one such unattributed segment which appears to fit none of these conventions. Rather, it appears to be constructed of a number of discrete layers within the unattributed sugya. Each layer has a different and very limited focus, such that the whole cannot be seen as a structured lecture, and it concedes too much to label each separately an academic lecture. Rather, the model I propose for this sugya, and implicitly for others as well, is of a literary development of the sugya in the hands not of senior scholars, but probably of senior students, whose interesting work was then passed on and glossed again in subsequent generations.[6]

---

[5]This tripartite division is characteristic of the work of D. Halivni, see the introductions to *Sources and Traditions, Yoma-Hagiga*, pp. 9-10, *Shabbat*, p. 12. Others lean in the same direction without expressly acknowledging the problem. Thus, for instance, Y. Efrati writes in his Hebrew book *The Period of the Savoraim and Its Literature*, p. 162, "What brought the expositors of the gemara (of the anonymous sugya)—even if (only) the latest of them, such as the Savoraic Rabbis...." (my trans.). I note, however, that S. Friedman, ibid., pp. 285-289, is careful not to posit different eras and judges, only differences in style. He sets aside from the normal unattributed material only those segments "which have a salient character and style...and which differ from the usual style in the gemara and are identifiable as a foreign entity in the flow of the sugya" (my trans.). To me it seems pertinent to add that according to the descriptions of Sherira Gaon in his letter (*Epistle of R. Sherira Gaon*, ed. B.M. Lewin, Frankfurt 1921; Jerusalem, 1972) and of *The Chronology of the Tannaim and Amoraim* (ed. K. Kahana, 1935), from which all historical descriptions of this period stem, there are only three periods in the development of Talmudic materials: the Amoraic, Savoraic and Geonic. On that basis, when one concludes that much of the unattributed Talmud is post-Amoraic it would seem that that should lead to a changed understanding of the work of the Savoraim, rather than to the construction of a new period, though there may well have been significant developments in style and substance between the beginning of that period and its end.

[6]To be sure, notice has been taken in the literature of some form of layering or later glossing within the unattributed Talmud itself. Thus H. Albeck writes, *Introduction to the Talmud, Babli and Yerushalmi* (Hebrew) (Tel Aviv, 1969), p. 591: "Thus we have found comments by the unattributed Talmud on an unattributed (passage) formulated earlier, when by our reckoning they are from different periods" (my trans.). See also D. Halivni, op. cit., *Shabbat*, pp. 5-6, on the first of Albeck's examples. These notices, however, are episodic and largely about short, single-entry glosses. This is consistent with the commentary model noted earlier.

The sugya in question, B. Shev. 3a-5a, is at heart a short Amoraic sugya, glossed front and back.[7] I shall focus only on the material preliminary to the Amoraic comments and dispense altogether with the latter sugya. I herewith provide a slightly abridged English version of the sugya through the Amoraic comments (translation my own).

M. Shev. 1:1:

Oaths are of two types, which yield four.

Awarenesses of impurity, of two types which yield four.

Removals on the Sabbath, of two types which yield four.

The symptoms of afflictions, of two types which yield four.

A)   According to whom is the Mishnah?   Not R. Ishmael and not R. Akiba.

For did R. Ishmael not say: "He is not liable except for (oaths about) the future"

And did R. Akiba not say: "He is liable for a lapse in (his awareness of) impurity, but he is not liable for a lapse in (his knowledge of) the Temple."

B)   One might say R. Ishmael, one might say R. Akiba.

One might say R. Ishmael: some are liabilities, some are exemptions

One might say R. Akiba: some are liabilities, some are exemptions.

—Exemptions?   Does the Mishnah not teach a parallel to symptoms of affliction?   Just as there all are liabilities, so here all must be liabilities!

C)   Withal, (it is according to) R. Ishmael.   Whereas R. Ishmael does not find one liable for a sacrifice in (oaths about) the past, he does indeed find one liable for lashes.

It should be noted that this author assumes the existence of commentatorial glosses as a feature of a total model. The latter model demonstrated here is, after all, not so different from the model of a Tosafot-like work, Tosafot also incorporating many layers of the glosses and suggestions of students and sages alike. It differs from that primarily in the freedom from constraint that is implicit in a free literary creation as opposed to a commentary. As will become evident, the primary layers of this sugya develop not out of a desire to comment on the text, but out of a broader desire to adorn it. One clear statement to that effect is that of Dr. Friedman in his substantive footnote on this subject (above, note 3). He writes: "Most of the unattributed discussion is a literary work by the author of the gemara. The very balanced and measured nature of the structure of the sugya leads to this conclusion" (my trans.).

[7] A. Weiss treats of this sugya at some length in *Notes to Sugyot of the Babylonian and Palestinian Talmuds* (Bar Ilan, no date), pp. 242-246, originally published in *Beit Shmuel* (Warsaw, 1937).

C')   In accord with Rava, for Rava says: "The Torah expressly included false oath parallel to vain (oath). Just as vain (oath) is about the past, so, too, false (oath) is about the past."

1.   Granted: 'I ate', and 'I did not eat'—these accord with Rava, 'I will not eat', but he ate—that is (transgression of) a negative precept actively, but 'I will eat', but he did not eat—Why? This is (a transgression of) a negative precept through inactivity (and should on that account be exempt from lashes)!?

—R. Ishmael holds that (transgression of) a negative precept through inactivity is punishable by lashes.

2.   If so do not R. Johanan's statements contradict? For R. Johanan says: "The law accords with the unattributed Mishnah." Yet it is said: "'I swear I shall eat this loaf today,' but the day passed and he did not.... R. Johanan says: He is not lashed because this is a negative precept (transgressed) through inactivity, and (transgression of) a negative precept through inactivity is not punishable by lashes."

—R. Johanan must have found a different unattributed Mishnah.

3.   Which unattributed Mishnah?

a.   If one says the unattributed Mishnah which teaches: "But he who leaves a remnant of the pure (Paschal sacrifice) and he who breaks (bones) in the impure does not receive the forty lashes"...why does he who leaves a remnant of the pure not (receive lashes)? Because it is a negative precept (transgressed) through inactivity, and (transgression of) a negative precept through inactivity is not punishable by lashes.

—On what basis (does one assume this accords with R. Jacob...perhaps it accords with R. Judah!?... For it is taught: " 'Let nothing remain...and the remnant...burn with fire.' —the verse intentionally places a positive precept after the negative in order to say that one does not receive lashes for it, the words of R. Judah. R. Jacob says: ...the reason (one does not receive lashes is) because this is a negative precept (transgressed) through inactivity, and (transgression of) a negative precept through inactivity is not punishable by lashes.

b.   Rather, he found this unattributed Mishnah: " 'I swear that I shall not eat this loaf, I swear I shan't eat it', but he ate it—he is only liable for one (sacrifice). This is a rash oath for which one is liable for lashes for intentional transgression, and for a variable sacrifice for unintentional transgression."— This is the one for which one is liable for lashes for intentional transgression, but " 'I will eat', but he did not eat" does not receive lashes.

4.   Since this is an unattributed Mishnah and so is the other, on what basis did (R. Johanan) act in accordance with this one and not that one?

—By that reasoning, how could Rabbi (Judah the Patriarch) himself leave unattributed a Mishnah here like this and there like that? Rather, originally (R. Judah) held that (transgression of) a negative precept through inactivity is punishable by lashes and left that unattributed, and he reversed himself and held that (transgression of) a negative precept through inactivity is not punishable by lashes and left that unattributed, but a Mishnah (once in place) is immutable.

D)   On what basis is (the Mishnah) established to be according to R. Ishmael with regard to lashes?

a.   In symptoms of affliction, what lashes are there?

—(There are) in (the case of) one who crops his white spot. In accord with R. Avin says R. Ila'a who says: "Wherever it says 'be vigilant', 'lest' and 'do not'—that is a negative precept."

b.   In removals on the Sabbath, what lashes are there?... Every negative precept punishable at court by death receives no lashes!?

—That is why I established (the Mishnah) according to R. Ishmael who says: "A negative precept punishable at court by death receives lashes."

....

c.   If so, "awarenesses"—(the Mishnah) needs (to read) 'warnings'!

—That is no problem.   The Mishnah teaches   'awarenesses' of 'warnings'.

If so, "two types which yield four"—there are only two!

Moreover, "if there is awareness at first and awareness at the end and a lapse in between"—what function has lapse with regard to lashes!?

Moreover, "This is (atoned) by a variable sacrifice"!

E)   Rather, Rav Joseph says: "It is according to Rabbi (Judah the Patriarch) who cast it in accordance with the teachers.   'Awarenesses' he cast in accord with R. Ishmael, 'oaths' he casts in accord with R. Akiba.

F)   Says Rav Ashi: I recited this lesson before Rav Kahana, who said to me, "Do not say Rabbi cast it in accordance with the teachers but did not hold so himself. Rather, Rabbi sets out his own reasoning."

This is the first basic sugya in this tractate, preceded only by two unattributed and apparently late segments dealing with certain ordinal and definitional issues in the Mishnah. The Mishnah, itself, is a classic collection based on a formula rather than a theme,[8] but the first two items also share the same source in Lev.

---

[8]See H. Albeck, *Introduction to the Mishna* (Hebrew) (Jerusalem 1959, reprint, 1979), pp. 88-89. Albeck departs from the standard interpretation that these formal collections represent an older form of Mishnah, preferring to see the difference as a matter of style. The more common view has been that these collections are older—thus N. Krochmal, *The Guide of the Perplexed of the Time* (ed. Rawidowicz, 1924), p. 208, Z. Frankel, *Introduction to the Mishnah* (Hebrew) (Warsaw 1923), p. 305, J. Lauterbach, "Midrash and Mishnah," *Rabbinic Essays* (1951), p. 177, and more recently, A. Goldberg, *Commentary to the Mishna: Shabbat* (Hebrew) (Jerusalem, 1976), p. 2, n. 2, and D. Halivni, *Studies in Rabbinic Literature, Bible and Jewish History* (1982), p. 108.

5, and thus both are treated in this tractate, and both counts are elaborated upon by the opening Mishnayot of the relevant sections ahead. As follows:

M. Shev. 1:1:
Oaths are of two types, which yield four.
Awarenesses of impurity, of two types which yield four.

M. Shev. 3:1:
Oaths are of two types, which yield four.
An oath that 'I will eat' and that 'I will not eat', that 'I ate' and that 'I did not eat'.

M. Shev. 2:1
Awarenesses of impurity are of two types which yield four.
He became impure and knew it, then forgot the impurity but remembered the sacred meat, or forgot the sacred meat but remembered his impurity, or forgot them both, and ate the sacred meat, not knowing, but after he ate he became aware, he brings a variable sacrifice.
He became impure and knew it, then forgot the impurity but remembered the sacred precinct, or forgot the sacred precinct but remembered his impurity, or forgot them both, and entered the sacred precinct, not knowing, but after he left he became aware, he brings a variable sacrifice.

Each of those elaborations is clearly counterindicated by another clause in the Mishnah, as cited by the sugya in section A,[9] which generates the theme question of this sugya: "According to whom is the Mishnah—it does not follow R. Ishmael nor does it follow R. Akiba?"

The sugya then develops as follows. Two suggestions to solve the discrepancy are offered and rejected by the unattributed sugya in B through D, then a third suggestion by the Amora Rav Yosef is upheld at E. The Talmud suggests first, in B, that the Mishnah might in fact follow either R. Ishmael or R. Akiba provided that we view the count as inclusive of cases in which one is exempt from the relevant offering. Next, in C, it is suggested that the whole Mishnah might, after all, be made to fit the ruling of R. Ishmael, thus: R. Ishmael's ruling that oaths about past actions are exempt comes in the context of a discussion of the duty to bring offerings for unintentional transgression. If we allow that R. Ishmael might hold a more restrictive view with regard to intentionally false oaths, then it would be possible to view the count as a count of cases of corporal punishment for intentional transgression according to R. Ishmael's view, rather than a count of offerings due for unintentional transgression. When that too is rejected the Talmud repairs to Rav Yosef's view, that the Mishnah is according to Rabbi (Judah the Patriarch), the compiler of the

---

[9]R. Ishmael's comment: M. Shev. 3:5, R. Akiba's comment: M. Shev. 2:5.

Mishnah, who chose to write the law in one case in accordance with R. Ishmael and in the other in accordance with R. Akiba.

On its face it is evident that we are dealing here with an Amoraic comment to the Mishnah—fully called for by the discrepancies in the Mishnah, and in no wise informed by the intervening unattributed material. The unattributed material was rather created in light of Rav Yosef's solution. As such, this unattributed sugya belongs to a class of unattributed preamble sugyot whose task is to cast the Amora's dictum in a rich context. In particular, this is of the genre of straw-man preambles, which propose preliminary hypotheses to be rejected in favor of the position which had been received in the Amoraic tradition. As such, the sugya seeks apparent analogies in other source material to support an analysis that differs from the received dicta. As such, also, fully supportable analogies are less desirable than false analogies which bear within them the seed of their own rejection.

This straw man sugya can itself be subdivided into different sections which either offer different hypotheses or consider different blocks of data with regard to the mooted hypotheses. It is extremely important to maintain the distinction between these sections because there is no intrinsic reason that the sections need be from the same hand or even period. Once the process of introducing straw men has begun there is no bar to later attempts to try one's hand at furthering the debate.[10] Yet it appears to me that the process of glossing contains within itself a tool to winnow the original unattributed sugya from its expansions. The perception of the initial formation of a preamble sugya would have been that a received and true tradition is to be illuminated by showing the many false trails the Amora unerringly avoided. The perception of the glossator, however, is very likely to be that he has an unassailable critique or a better hypothesis than was advanced before him. The impetus to annotate is in outdoing the text. Thus where the original formulation should prefer pitfalls that one might easily be lead into, but whose flaws are inherent and accessible, the glosses should tend toward unassailable thrusts, often intricately conceived, which are parried only weakly, though parry we must since ultimately the Amora must prevail.

---

[10]A clear example of such extraneous glossing is noted by Rashi and Tosafot. Rashi rejects the gloss as a student's error, while Tosafot defends it. Tosafot's defense is in turn built upon Rabbenu Hananel's solution to a question similar to that of the gloss, which question he does not have before him, but appears to introduce in his commentary *ad locum*. Thus there is little question that the additional question in the Talmud is the result of a gloss, which accounts for the absence of an answer to said question in the text and for certain peculiarities of its phrasing.

The lead question, "According to whom is the Mishnah", is an agent of the unattributed Talmud,[11] which, together with its expansion in A, sets out in detail

---

[11] That the question is, here, an agent of the unattributed sugya is not perfectly evident on its face. The general question of whether short questions which serve as openings to Amoraic dicta were sometimes part of the received Amoraic traditions or are necessarily later fabrications has been a vexed question among the scholars. Albeck, *Introduction to the Talmud*, p. 578, n. 4, writes: "In places where the question is unattributed and the answer in the name of an Amora, it goes without saying that the question is no later than the time of that Amora" (my trans.). But his opinion should be treated cautiously because he did not accept the premise that as a rule the unattributed Talmud is post-Amoraic, and because he himself perceived numerous exceptions to his own rule (ibid., p. 510ff.). S. Friedman (op. cit., p. 296-299) stands against Albeck and implies that all unattributed questions should be considered post-Amoraic, barring specific proof to the contrary. He aligns himself firmly with H. Klein ("Gemara and Sebara", *JQR* 38 (1947), pp. 67-91), who establishes (p. 91) that: "The question which an Amoraic interpretation purports to answer must be looked upon as a construction of later date than the answer." But Klein, too, must be construed cautiously, for his case examples are all of long complex questions which form a part of the backbone of give and take which is the essence of the unattributed layer of the Talmud. It is precisely of short, direct questions of a form which would be suitable to the Amoraic transmission that this question is relevant.

D. Halivni leans toward the position of Albeck, with appropriate caution. He formulates his position thus (op. cit., *Yoma-Hagiga*, p. 9): "The unattributed questions which come...before Amoraic answers...are not true stamot. They *may be* the words of the Amoraim which the Talmud arranged anonymously for reasons of style alone" (my trans. and emphasis. My elipsis masks a significant change of meaning, but see the continuation of the passage and Halivni's own citation thereof in *Eruvin*, p. 189, n. 1).

To date, I know of no careful tests of specific short questions to determine if they were an integral part of the Amoraic transmission. On its face the notion is not far-fetched, for such a format allows the collation of dicta said separately under one heading, as is often the case with the statement of law in a Mishnah and is equally the norm in the Amoraic collations under the rubric of *'tmr*

To return to the issue at hand, the preliminary stage of a full analysis of the usage of the terms *"mny mtnytyn," "mny", "h' mny,"* and *"m'n tn',"* strongly suggests that the latter two terms are regularly associated with Amoraic material, while the former correlate with the unattributed material in the Talmud. While it is difficult to assume that the latter terms were always the initial formulation of the Amora, the strong correlation suggests that they were either the formulation of the tradents of the period or a very early editorial feature, before the development of the characteristic features of the unattributed Talmud. Were the standardization of this feature any later, it is highly unlikely that it would not suffer significant variation in manuscript and indeed that it would not be known and remarked upon by the classical commentators. It is therefore safe to state that the question *mny*

the parameters of the problem that the straw men and Rav Yosef tackle. Since Rav Yosef finds the Mishnah disjoint, a solution which only serves to confirm the problem, the unattributed sugya has a challenge, in addition to the normal business of highlighting Rav Yosef's solution, to show the exclusivity of that solution, that is, that there is no more conservative solution available.

The first straw man, then, is mooted and rejected in B. The hypothesis: that the Mishnah's count may include exempt behavior. Thus the perceived clash between the count in the Mishnah and the positions of either R. Akiba or R. Ishmael is null. The rejection: 1) that the very nature of the Mishnah which collects like cases of "two types yielding four," demands that the cases be fully analogous, and 2) the notion of including exempt behavior is not possible with regard to symptoms of affliction wherein the subject is a condition, not a behavior, and all the symptoms demand a sacrifice of purification.

Both the hypothesis and the retort have their sources in an unattributed expansion to an upcoming Amoraic sugya on B. Shev. 5a.[12] There, Rav Pappa compares the counts in the Mishnayot with regard to removals on the Sabbath, M. Shab. 1:1 and M. Shev. 1:1, and concludes that the Mishnah of Shevuot counts only liabilities whereas that of Shabbat includes also exemptions. Pappa's dictum would seem to rule out this hypothesis here, and indeed it does, (a straw man needs to be flawed), but in fact it is not upon his dictum that our sugya builds, but upon an unattributed preamble which accompanies his dictum and serves as its straw man. In considering the straw man to Rav Pappa the unattributed sugya adopts Pappa's own system that exemptions may be counted in a Mishnah and suggests that even the lesser count of removals on the Sabbath found in M. Shev. includes exemptions. This must perforce be rejected in favor of Pappa's reading, which it is, under the rationale that an analogy must be maintained to symptoms of affliction. The wording of both the straw man and its rejection in our sugya is virtually identical.

There is room to hesitate in assigning one unattributed sugya priority over the other. But it appears probable that the source is the latter sugya, since the essential notion that a Mishnah might count exemptions along with liabilities derives from Rav Pappa's dictum there. Furthermore, a suggestion propounded in direct opposition to Pappa might reasonably take the view that if Pappa finds the distinction between the Mishnayot of Shevuot and Shabbat in the counting or discounting of exemptions, then a contrary view must count exemptions in

---

mtnytyn is an agent of the unattributed sugya without prejudicing that judgement with regard to other short questions that have not yet been studied.

[12]See appendix A.

both (no one suggests a way to reach Shabbat's count without including them). But here, what sense does it make to extend to oaths and awarenesses of impurity in M. Shev. Pappa's reasoning with regard to Sabbath removals as counted in M. Shab. when he expressly rejects such a count for Sabbath removals in the present context? Rather, it appears that the suggestion in this sugya bases itself directly on the rejected proposition in the latter sugya, which claimed both exemptions and liabilities in the Sabbath count in M. Shev., whereby it is reasonable to extend such a count to the other clauses in that Mishnah. Thus the presentation of the straw man and its retort are an integral package, here.[13]

The rest of this unattributed straw man sugya is all subsumed under the second straw man, C, although the passage is complex. Unpacking the sugya will allow easier access to its form, assumptions and sources. The second straw man focuses attention on the case of oaths which was taken to be problematic for R. Ishmael. The hypothesis: Throughout the Mishnayot of oaths there is a parallel treatment of the differing rules regarding intentional and unintentional transgressions.[14] Since the inconsistency in the count resides in the rulings about unintentional transgressions for which one brings an offering, perhaps the Mishnah could be taken to be counting the intentional transgressions for which one is lashed. As in the first straw man, the hypothesis is available on the face of the data under consideration. The retort does not follow directly, however. C' is fully susceptible to bracketing. The direct retort begins at D, and it, like the previous retort, is predicated on the need to interpret all the clauses of this Mishnah consistently. The retort: If the clause on oaths is now to be taken as dealing with the cases which are punishable by lashes, then each of the other clauses needs to be susceptible to a reading as a count of instances which are punishable by lashes. The sugya proceeds to test all three and finds such a

---

[13]The specifics of the retort here also suggest that it had its origins in the expansion of the latter sugya. Were this sugya to precede that expansion, it would yet be technically possible to construct this question on the basis of Pappa's dictum there by splitting his dictum. Accepting his statement that both liabilities and exemptions are counted with regard to removals on the Sabbath in Mishnah Shabbat, it is vaguely conceivable that this unattributed gemara might try to extend that principle in the abstract to the other clauses of Mishnah Shevuot—neglecting momentarily that in the latter part of his dictum Pappa rejects that idea with regard to Sabbath removals there. Were that the case, however, the fatal flaw of the proposition should be the juxtaposition of oaths and awarenesses of impurity to Sabbath removals wherein Rav Pappa himself had already ruled against that interpretation, rather than their juxtaposition to symptoms of affliction. That example belongs to the attempt to introduce Pappa's dictum in the latter sugya.

[14]M. Shev. 3:7-8, 3:10-11, 4:2, 5:1.

reading inconsistent with the language of the clause regarding awareness of impurity.[15] Thus this second straw man also fails, leaving the way clear for Rav Yosef.

The intermediate section nested within the second straw man is primarily a consideration of information available in this tractate concerning the laws of lashes for intentional transgression of the laws of oaths. In chapter 3, on 20b-21a, is an Amoraic sugya with an additional collection of Amoraic materials on that subject, collected, revised and explicated by the unattributed gemara.[16] The citation of Rava at C', the analysis reported under "Granted" at C'1, the ruling in

---

[15]There is a peculiarity in the text of the retort which causes the commentators some consternation. I deleted the offensive turn in my transcript of the sugya, above, between Db and Dc. There follows upon Db a parenthetical gloss, as follows:

—Were it not for that, would it (the Mishnah) be established according to R. Akiba? Awareness of impurity remains a problem! Did you not say that it is according to R. Ishmael with regard to lashes? So, too, according to R. Akiba with regard to lashes!

Rashi properly takes this as a parenthetical comment, which no doubt arose in response to that uncommon first person usage in Db. Thus also in the novellae of Nahmanides (Ramban), Solomon ben Abraham Adret (Rashba) and Yom-Tov ben Abraham Ishbili (Ritba). But a sequential reading of the text with the gloss inserted poses very real problems. Read that way, the follow up in Dc appears to be addressed to the view that the Mishnah is according to R. Akiba, not R. Ishmael. This reading is essayed by the Tosafot on 4a, and in the novellae of Nissim Gerondi (Ran), and by A. Weiss, *Notes*, p. 244, who finds this an example of stream of consciousness argumentation which is "the result of live discussion" (my trans.).

This is, however, impossible. Not only does this prematurely terminate the review of the three clauses of the Mishnah in light of the proposition that the Mishnah accords with R. Ishmael with regard to lashes, but it effectively completes the discussion with an unnecessary rejection of the proposition that the Mishnah is according to R. Akiba with regard to lashes (he has already failed the test of the prior clause) and leaves the major proposition, that the Mishnah might be according to R. Ishmael with regard to lashes, unanswered. This runs counter to every tenet of a straw man preamble, for it leaves Rav Yosef's comment as an uncalled-for and excessively radical solution.

Clearly this is a parenthetical gloss to the unusual first person language in Db, which language may itself represent a copyist's gloss intended to call attention to a potential reason why the sugya seems to seek to parse the Mishnah in accordance with R. Ishmael rather than in accordance with the generally dominant position of R. Akiba.

[16]See appendix B.

the name of Johanan at C'2 and the Mishnah analysis at C'3b all have their source in that sugya.

The jump-off point for this infix is the desire to back up the hypothesis that the count of the Mishnah of cases of oaths may be taken to accord to the view of R. Ishmael and to refer to cases which are punishable by lashes. The source sugya is the primary discussion of that subject, and the backup is taken from a dictum of Rava's there.[17] There are three flaws. Rava's dictum provides no information on R. Ishmael's position, leaving open the likelihood that Ishmael, who rejects sacrifices for unintentional transgression in retrospective oaths, would not support lashes for intentional transgression in that case either. If the proof is only that there exists an opinion that requires lashes in that case,

---

[17]Most manuscripts read Rava here and in the source sugya on 21a and again in a parallel on Temurah 3b. The geniza fragment TS AS 75.90 and R. Hananel, however, read Rabbah here, though Hananel then reads Rava on 21a. The interchange of Rava and Rabbah in manuscript is quite common, with all such interchanges of the alef/heh ending. Additionally, Florence reads Rav on 21a, but the text there is corrupt in a number of regards. The two sages lived near enough in time that this is often not a sufficient criterion to determine a proper reading. Thus here, in the base sugya Rava's dictum is brought in response to R. Abbahu's analysis. Considering the normal modes of transmission, a third generation Palestinian analysis would comfortably receive a fourth generation Babylonian gloss (Rava), but it cannot be said that a third generation response (Rabbah) is impossible. Moreover, it is not at all clear that the dictum on 21a was in fact composed in light of Abbahu's analysis, and it may simply have been placed in that context in the course of the editing of that sugya. There is thus no conclusive evidence as to the correct reading here. The possibility that the geniza fragment is older and maintains the correct reading cannot be gainsaid, however older manuscripts are also known to be less meticulous in such vagaries of spelling.

Dr. S. Friedman has pointed out to me that in certain manuscripts of Bava Metzia, there appears to be a development from non-differentiation of Rava/Rabbah in certain old manuscripts to a later attempt to determine the sage in question by differentiation of the spelling of the name of the sage, as we have grown accustomed to do. If TS AS 75.90 is from such a "careful" manuscript, then it may indeed be affirmative evidence of a "ruling" that the sage in question was the third generation Rabbah. I do not have evidence of the nature of the manuscript from which this fragment derives, however, nor do I have specific reason to posit that the other manuscripts and editions, all of which are familiar with the distinction of spelling, derive from an undifferentiating prototype. Note too that the reading chosen by the anonymous copyist of a "careful" manuscript, though carrying significant weight, is not of itself unimpeachable evidence of the sage whose dictum is recorded. Ultimately, only internal evidence is probative, here. Given the information available in this case, I believe that the preponderant reading is to be preferred.

leaving the reader to assume that R. Ishmael agrees on that point, there is no need to seek backup in the gemara—that is clearly stated in the Mishnah.[18] Moreover, if the attempt is to show the law in its relation to Scripture, there are several better citations in the source sugya.[19] This, too, is a clue to the thinking of the sugya's crafter. Rava's dictum is presented on 21a as the final response in the primary sugya on the subject of lashes for oaths. The author of the infix here treats Rava's dictum as a summary of that sugya, representing the sum of the information generated by the discussion there, not simply the information conveyed in his own words. R. Ishmael, it is assumed absent evidence to the contrary, concurs with the established ruling.

The infix continues to explore the ramifications of the information in its source in chapter 3. If the Mishnah is correctly readable as a count of cases of lashes, then all four enumerated cases, "I will eat, I will not eat, I ate, I did not eat", need to be cases which draw lashes. But an analysis by R. Abbahu there allows lashes in only three of the four cases. This is based on rulings by R. Johanan that false oaths, wherein the transgression is simply speaking, are punishable by lashes, but in the case of transgression through inactivity ("I will eat", but did not), no lashes are incurred. This poses a problem for the proposed hypothesis which the infix now addresses, without citing the source of its analysis, though it is R. Abbahu's analysis verbatim. However, since the author

---

[18]M. Shev. 3:1 lists "'I will eat' and 'I will not eat', 'I ate' and 'I did not eat.'" These are the rash oaths (literally: uttered oaths) which are ruled punishable by lashes in M. 3:7, or else they might be classed as vain oaths, as per the opinion of Rav Dimi citing R. Johanan on 20b and of Rav Isaac bar Avin on 26a, which are also punishable by lashes. It is only an unattributed expansion of the position of R. Jeremiah on 21b that considers the possibility that retrospective oaths might be exempt from punishment as negative precepts transgressed through inactivity, a position nowhere evident in the sources. See note 22 below. (It is expressly only Ishmael, of whom the sugya speaks, who might hold retrospective oaths exempt from lashes, as he sees them exempt from the sacrifice, and one certainly cannot gauge his opinion by reference to the normative one.)

[19]Both the dictum of Rav Dimi in the name of R. Johanan, "'I ate' and 'I did not eat' are vain oaths and their prohibition (is derived) from here..." and that of Ravin that stands opposed are relevant. Tosafot, 3b s.v. *kdrb'*, prefers yet another dictum of R. Johanan to support the hypothesis. Indeed, Rava's dictum does not expressly deal with the liability for lashes for intentional transgression of the law of oaths at all. Rather it deals with the types of oaths and their time-frames, a model which may be applied to unintentional transgression as well as intentional. Of this, too, see the aforementioned Tosafot and compare the speculations of the unattributed sugya in comparing vain and false oaths at the bottom of 20b and the top of 21a.

of the infix[20] knows this to be a ruling by an Amora, it does not present a significant challenge to a hypothesis about the views of a Tanna. The sugya asserts, in defense of the hypothesis, that Ishmael would have ruled to the contrary in the case of transgression through inactivity. This step eliminates the challenge to the hypothesis and the sugya could now proceed to the retort to the hypothesis, but that the author of the infix has a further problem to consider based on the source in chapter 3.[21]

The second problem is an apparent contradiction between R. Johanan's position as recorded in chapter 3 and a general position he is known to hold. This second challenge tips the author's hand, for it depends on the knowledge that the analysis above is attributable to R. Johanan, a datum not provided in this sugya, but evident in the source in chapter 3. In order to document the question, the sugya has to produce Johanan's stated position, so it introduces another piece of its source material here, in C'2, stating in R. Johanan's name that "(transgression of) a negative precept through inactivity is not punishable by lashes." The apparent contradiction: If Johanan is expected to rule with the unattributed Mishnah, as a well-known dictum of his asserts, then how did he rule against this Mishnah, as it has now been interpreted in accordance with the hypothecated position of R. Ishmael that lashes are given for transgression through inactivity?

In order to solve this contradiction without abandoning the hypothesis it is necessary to find R. Johanan an unattributed Mishnah to stand against this one in support of his position on lashes for inactivity. That search for a suitable Mishnaic source for his datum turns up one dry hole and a solution. This is the nesting phenomenon. The solution is necessary to the conclusion of this segment of the sugya, the failed attempt could be just that, or could itself be a straw man provided at a later date. Unpacking, I start with the solution. Not surprisingly, the solution found in C'3b is itself a Mishnah, explicated in line with the position of R. Johanan in the source sugya.[22]

---

[20]I presume to speak of one author here, although I have not yet shown that the new beginning is not a gloss by another hand. My position will become clear anon.

[21]Perhaps this may be generalized. The unattributed gemara may be expected to present backup texts in verbatim attributed form since its own dicta do not carry the weight to support other constructs. Where it is its analysis which is derivative, however, it will not call attention to that fact, presumably, since the strength of the analysis rests not an authority but on logical weight.

[22]The explication, embedded in a question posed by R. Jeremiah, appears to be worked by the unattributed editor of the sugya there. It is, of course, impossible to go into that sugya in detail, here, but a quick rehearsal is of value. The sugya

This weaving of threads from a single source sugya attests to a unified infix whose author controlled both the questions and answers. When he supports the straw man hypothesis from there, he knows that there is a problem with the count. When he proposes a justification of the count in accordance with R. Ishmael he knows that this leaves a problem for R. Johanan. And when he highlights the contradiction in R. Johanan's position, he knows that its solution is at hand. This is certainly not a live give and take, but rather a subtle, contrived presentation of a body of peripheral information not relevant to the

---

is based upon two competing dicta brought to Babylonia by Rav Dimi and Ravin, each in the name of R. Johanan. These attempt to clarify the Biblical verses concerning oaths. The primary difference between them is whether retrospective oaths are to be classed as false oaths (the intentional counterpart of unintentional rash oaths) or as vain oaths, because they cannot possibly be fulfilled. The difference at law between these positions will be whether a sacrifice is due for an unintentional transgression. Rav Pappa comments upon Ravin's version of R. Johanan, among whose tradents is R. Abbahu, that it was not said expressly, but deduced from other material by Johanan and Abbahu. There follows a question by R. Jeremiah of R. Abbahu.

The sugya as it stands interprets R. Jeremiah's question as a question at law challenging Abbahu on his analysis as brought by Pappa. That implies that the question was originally asked not in this immediate context, for Pappa introduced the material here in the following generation. And Jeremiah's question is odd. He asks if there is, in fact, a punishment of lashes for retrospective oaths, when that appears to be the evident meaning of the Mishnah and of the lead Amoraic dicta of this sugya (see footnote 18 above). Nor are his inferences clear. The Mishnah provides for two classes of oaths, whereby one might ask, as do the dicta of Johanan that head the sugya, whether a particular item is to be classed as one or the other. Jeremiah seeks to infer to a class that is neither.

The explication of Jeremiah's question, therefore, appears to be unattributed and in error. Jeremiah's conversation with Abbahu can better be understood with regard to the primary subject of the sugya. Abbahu/Johanan classed retrospective oaths as false oaths in the lead dictum. Jeremiah attempts to challenge that classification by inference from the beginning of M. 3:7. It follows that Abbahu retorted that the opposite inference might be made from the latter clause in that Mishnah. (Those words are presented in the present gemara as a second question by R. Jeremiah, but absent the interpretation of the unattributed explicator and they would have to devolve back to Abbahu). Thus the debate of R. Jeremiah and R. Abbahu gets to the heart of the ambiguity out of which the two versions of R. Johanan grew. (R. Jeremiah himself is cited as a conveyor of the Abbahu/Johanan tradition—perhaps Abbahu convinced him). The sugya editor, however, was influenced by the intervening material supplied by Rav Pappa in the next generation and essayed an explanation of that debate based on that material and not the original subject matter at hand.

conclusions of the sugya. This infix, like the straw men into which it is set, expands the discussion but does not advance it.

I have discussed two blocks of unattributed material, the pair of straw men and the infix based on chapter three. One more block remains, that is the failed support text for R. Johanan nested within the infix. The failed source appears twice, M. Pes. 7:11 and M. Mak. 3:3. The surrounding discussion focuses on a baraita associated with this Mishnah *in situ* on B. Pes. 84a, which is also found on B. Mak. 4b and 16a, the latter in association with Johanan's dictum. Johanan's position is represented in the baraita by R. Jacob, who finds that to be the reasoning behind the ruling in the Mishnah, but R. Judah presents a different reasoning. The sugya presents Jacob's understanding of the Mishnah as Johanan's Mishnaic source, in unattributed form. It finds that that is an insufficient source for Johanan, however, since the Mishnah's reasoning is a matter of debate. Again, it appears clear from the question, in C'3a, "How can we know that the reasoning of the Mishnah is that of R. Jacob", when the text had been introduced in unattributed form, and from the fact that this Mishnah and baraita are a clear package, that this too is a straw man, contrived to present an additional text coyly. In this instance, however, the text comes from without the source sugya of the infix, and we will need to establish whence it was drawn.

To review, this sugya, up to the Amoraic comments of Rav Yosef and Rav Kahana is made up of the following blocks:

1) the presentation and explication of the question facing the Amoraim, which serves as a preamble and bridge to the straw men that the sugya wishes to propose—A

2) two straw men used to set up the definitive solution to the question which was reported in the name of Rav Yosef—B,C,D

3) an infix within the second straw man working the implications of information from one sugya in chapter 3 of this tractate—C', and

4) a short secondary infix with reference to material from another source— C'3a.

It is necessary to consider if these are all the product of one author or rescension, or whether the unattributed sugya, itself, is the product of successive rescensions.

The explication of the Amoraic question could antedate the expansions, but it serves a well-defined purpose as introduction to the straw men, and there is no advantage to positing an additional stage in the development of the sugya. The two straw men themselves could, theoretically, be independent one of the other, but the fact that both focus on the need to interpret all the Mishnah's clauses consistently suggests that they were composed jointly.[23] The infix, however, appears to be a second stage. It performs a task which is not necessary for the presentation and rejection of the straw men. Indeed, it seeks to support a hypothesis which the straw man sugya sets out to present and reject. It should be noted, however, that part of the hypothesis posed in the second straw man, that R. Ishmael rules that lashes apply in the case of retrospective oaths, is in fact asserted in the sugya in chapter 3, apparently for internal reasons.[24] Withal, the fact that the ultimate rejection of the second straw man is based on the same concept as the rejection of the first, deriving from this chapter, and not on any ramification of the material from chapter three suggests to me that the author of the second straw man did not himself repair to the material there.

Whether the secondary infix comes from yet another source or is simply testimony to the tendency of the author of the infix to expand is a question which requires further elucidation. Nor have I yet determined the particular source from which the secondary infix is drawn. The information which controls these questions arises unexpectedly from a consideration of the complicated final rejection of the second straw man, in D.

The second straw man raised the hypothesis that the Mishnah is to be interpreted as counting cases of transgressions of oaths which are punishable by lashes. This is rejected by reviewing the other clauses of the Mishnah to see if they, too, can support such an interpretation, a review predicated on the theory of analogy of the Mishnah clauses. Yet that theory is not explicitly mentioned, and the testing of each of the three clauses is quite an elaborate structure, perhaps needlessly so for the simple refutation of a straw man. Therefore, it is well to consider if there has not been some expansion here, as well. There is no apparent seam in the text before us, so any tampering would appear to have been a substitution rather than a simple expansion. Such a substitution is much harder to verify. Nevertheless, I am inclined to suggest that initially a perfect parallel to the first retort should have been proposed here, thus:

> It must be analogous to symptoms of affliction, just as that refers to sacrifices, so here it refers to sacrifices.

---

[23] A weak suggestion, scholiasts often mimic. Nonetheless, in the absence of an indication to the contrary it is preferable to posit one unit.

[24] If this were so, then we should take the second straw man—and possibly the first as well—as completely formed by the author who introduced the material from chapter three, despite the appearance that material gives of being a lengthy digression. However, the layering of this sugya appears to me to be too clear a feature to disregard whereas the unattributed explication of R. Jeremiah in the sugya on 21a-b is very complex and shows some signs of being very late. See above, note 22. Much more needs to be said with regard to the sugya there.

Just as including exemptions failed because affliction is a condition, not a behavior from whose consequences one can be exempt, similarly it is impossible to speak of intentional transgression with regard to affliction, so no rule of lashes is applicable to symptoms of affliction. And this correlates particularly well with Sabbath removals, which are part of the forty less one labors of Shabbat whose count is attributed to the relevant sacrifices, and to oaths and awarenesses of impurity which are associated in Torah and this tractate of Mishnah because of their common sacrifice.[25]

If this is correct, then it is also obvious what led to the substitution. We deal here not with an expansion, but with a critical gloss. The simple parallel construction was quashed by a scholiast's observation that there does, in fact, exist a case of lashes found in the literature with regard to symptoms of affliction. That, then, motivated an abandonment of the *prima facie* retort in favor of the case by case test which follows. By my straw man test, suggested above, that straw men should be straightforward hypotheses with a clear flaw, the provision of cases to defend the hypothesis is a red flag warning of the entry of a gloss into the basic sugya.[26]

---

[25]An alternative reconstruction might be that the retort was originally from the need to be similar to awarenesses of impurity rather than to symptoms of affliction, with its traces remaining in the language testing on that case in the conclusion of the second straw man. It might be noted that the phrase *trty hw' dhwyyn* is also drawn from the sugya on 5a whence the retorts to the straw men are drawn. But this reconstruction does not read as well. In order to support this reconstruction it would be necessary to revise my consideration of the motive of the glossator, discussed below. The glossator would then seem to be offering potential retorts that fail. This is simply not as satisfying a reconstruction as I suggest in the body of this paper.

The commentators, here, seek reasons to prefer the analogy to symptoms of affliction to any analogy from another clause. Thus Tosafot, Rosh, Joseph haLevi Ibn Migash, Ramban, Rashba, Ritba and Ran. I am also so inclined, for the reasons presented in the body of the paper.

[26]Again, the language of the Talmud testifies to the fact that questions and their retorts are units, and not the product of live give and take, and that the intent of the glossator differs from that of the author of the straw men. The question at D, "On what basis..." is the opening to a retort. The question at Da, "What lashes are there?", while ostensibly a rhetorical question which completes the retort (there are no cases of lashes here, so, the hypothesis must be wrong), is phrased as a question, rather than being a simple assertion of fact, as an opening to the finding that there is, actually, such a case. Thus the ostensible retort to the hypothesis of the straw man has already been turned to the service of what's ahead, that is the glossator's attempt to defend the hypothesis which the author of the straw man wishes to abandon.

Whence does the author of the gloss draw the case which provokes his critical gloss and the other information in his case by case analysis? For the clause of symptoms of affliction, wherein the nature of the subject does not readily allow an intentional transgression, the glossator discovers a subsidiary case of transgression, where the patient sought to mislead the priests by removing the symptom of his affliction. The choice of the detailed "crops his white spot", however, is surprising. The relevant passage, M. Neg. 7:4 uses a general term, "detaches the symptoms of impurity." Similarly, the more expansive T. Neg. 3:1-2 writes:

"If he detaches the symptoms of impurity, tears an affliction from cloth or peels it from a house—he receives forty lashes."

Clearly neither of these obvious sources was the primary source for the terminology used by the author of this segment of our sugya. But both the Mishnah and the Tosefta testify to the existence of Tannaitic texts which focused not on the generalization which both present, but precisely on cropping a white spot. Both texts in their continuations in M. 7:5 and T. 3:5 refer to one who was afflicted with a discoloration and intentionally cut it off. They do not discuss the case in terms of a simple determination of liability, that being included in the general case. Rather, two subsidiary problems are addressed, 1) how to determine the time that the affliction has passed in the absence of the symptom and 2) whether cutting off the discoloration should be permitted in the course of circumcision.[27] These do not represent a fully satisfactory source for the usage in this sugya.

It is not necessary, however, to posit that the author of this late gloss referred to some other Tannaitic source, no longer extant. On B. Mak. 22a, in

---

[27]Both these problems concern cheating the system. In the former the concern is attempting to fool the priest monitoring the progress of the affliction, in the latter, to benefit through the circumcision by removing the discoloration. This latter situation is documented in the midrashic literature in Sifra, Tazria 1.4, and that appears as a baraita on B. Shab. 132b and in Y. Nedarim 3:9. In B. Shab. 133a there is an Amoraic proviso that, were the white spot removed during the normal course of the circumcision he could not be found to transgress, since one who does not willfully transgress is exempt, therefore, the beraita's concern can only apply where he has expressed his intention to be rid of the discoloration.

A. Weiss, *Notes*, p. 244, takes this as the source for the information in this sugya, but it is not sufficient. No reference to the nature of the punishment is to be found in these sources, all of them remaining well within the framework of the Mishnah in Negaim. In each case it is necessary to refer back to that Mishnah for the basic statement of liability for lashes for intentional transgression in such a case. A much better source is at hand.

discussing a Mishnah which attempts to construct a situation in which multiple transgressions are committed with one act,[28] a series of Amoraim add additional transgressions which could also be joined to the eight listed in the Mishnah. One of these, R. Abbahu, makes the following suggestion:

wlḥṣwb nmy hqwṣṣ 't bhrtw, w'zhrtyh mhk': hŝmr bngᶜ hṣrᶜt

Here is "one who crops his white spot" precisely in the context of general liability established by the verse term "*hŝmr.*" Only the R. Avin citation is absent there, and it is general, well-known, and, more to the point, utilized, albeit by the unattributed sugya, in the selfsame chapter on B. Mak. 13b.[29] Thus the source of the gloss appears to be chapter three of Makkot.

The difficulty finding a case of lashes with regard to Shabbat offenses rests on a general principle with regard to the proper application of lashes, namely that an offense punishable by death cannot be punished by lashes. Since Shabbat offenses are capital offenses, they cannot qualify for lashes. Here, the glossator asserts that R. Ishmael, putative author of our Mishnah, does not accept that principle. This is a perfect fingerprint. The principle is utilized by unattributed gemarot across the Talmud without dispute, but it is represented in an Amoraic sugya only once, where Rava reports it to be a point in dispute between R. Akiba and R. Ishmael—on B. Mak. 13b.[30]

---

[28]See M. Mak. 3:9

[29]The original locus in the Talmud of this general dictum by R. Avin is to be in this third chapter of Makkot which deals with the general data about negative precepts and their punishment, even though, in the Talmud as it stands, he is brought by the unattributed sugya. His dictum appears nine times in the Talmud— B. Eruv. 96a, Sot. 5a, Shev. 4a and 36a, Mak. 13b, A.Z. 51b, Zeb. 106a, Men. 36b and 99b—but nowhere is it stated directly. Rather it is always brought by unattributed sugyot (though some are immediate supports to Amoraic comments and might conceivably be part of Amoraic transmission). None of these offers itself as the source of the dictum, and it is my assumption that it has its origins in the material revolving around this chapter of Mishnah and its related midrash. See the following note.

[30]The principle that "every negative precept punishable at court by death receives no lashes" appears twice with regard to Sabbath laws, on B. Shab. 155a and B. Eruv. 17b, but those do not appear to be the source for this usage in Shevuot because only in Makkot is R. Ishmael's position mentioned, and the glossator is already utilizing Makkot. Furthermore, both instances in Shabbat and Eruvin are themselves unattached unattributed glosses, not integrally part of their surroundings.

It is interesting that in Eruvin an Amora, Aha bar Jacob, attacks a baraita of the school of R. Hiyya that prescribes lashes for transgression of Sabbath boundaries on the basis of a principle that no lashes are given for a negative

In light of this information that a glossator using materials from the third chapter of Makkot worked on this sugya, we can solidly identify the source and authorship of the secondary infix in the second straw man which question I had reserved. The Mishnaic source of that infix appears, as we said, in Pesahim and Makkot, on 17a in chapter three. Similarly, the associated baraita appears in full on B. Pes. 84a and B. Mak. 4b (the first chapter), and in part, without the crucial view of R. Jacob, on B. Mak. 16a. While Pesahim could serve as a source, the connection to Makkot and to the third chapter is evident.[31] Yet the baraita does not appear there in full, and the sugya context there, on 16a, is unattributed, late and problematic.[32] Thus if Makkot is the source, the source for the baraita would appear on its face to be the sugya on 4b, somewhat farther afield. The problem, however, is only apparent. On 4b the baraita including R. Jacob is

---

precept prescribed by "*l*." (So, also, in Y. Eruv. 3:4.) This assumption ties into the dictum of R. Avin. Are these sugyot hints of the existence of a collection of principles with regard to lashes or to negative precepts which circulated separately from the text of the Talmud *per se*?

[31] A. Weiss remarks in his monograph on the Savoraim, *Opus*, p. 13, that the source of this material is in Pesahim. But the note is based on the *prima facie* finding of the material there without a searching analysis.

[32] B. Mak. 16a does not appear to be the source of this sugya for several reasons. It brings the baraita only partially, without the position of R. Jacob which is central to the sugya here. Furthermore, the sugya there correlates R. Johanan's position with that of R. Judah in the baraita as opposed to the understanding of this gemara. But that sugya is an unattributed expansion, and odd in some fundamental ways. The primary sugya there deals with the problem of a negative precept that is followed directly by an associated positive command—can one exempt oneself from punishment by fulfilling the attached commandment. The sugya on 15b, "The Tanna taught before R. Johanan: A negative precept that has associated with it a positive command, if one fulfilled the associated positive command...", has its direct continuation on 16a, "It was taught there: He who takes the mother (bird) from among the children..." The intervening material attempting to explicate the positions of R. Johanan and Resh Lakish is a parenthetical expansion and may be quite late. One such sign, it has rather extensive variants—see Lehem Mishneh on Maimonides, San. 18:2.

And it is extremely problematic. On its face it is hard to understand how the sugya can associate R. Johanan with R. Judah when he so clearly matches Judah's opposite number, and applied to our sugya that association would ruin the putative second unattributed Mishnah which our sugya hopes to find in 3a. Indeed, the problems of that sugya are manifold and I shall not go into them here. Suffice it to say that the sugya there is clearly an insert and not the source of the sugya here. A much better source for our sugya is available in the original Amoraic materials of the third chapter of Makkot.

brought in secondary association with a dictum of Ulla's which belongs in that native context. The sugya there reports that "others teach Ulla's dictum with regard to the following" citing our baraita. Those who so taught certainly did so not in the context of the first chapter, but rather in connection with the Mishnah in chapter three. There is, therefore, no doubt that the material on 4b is part of the original Talmud to chapter three, and there is further no doubt that this addendum is the work of the glossator who applied his knowledge of the third chapter of Makkot to this sugya.

Thus we complete the picture of a sugya built of layers with each layer concerned with a single body of material, and with each successive layer further from the Mishnah being elucidated. The Amoraic sugya, here, consisted solely of the Amoraic comments of Yosef and Ashi/Kahana.[33] In the first layer of unattributed expansion, a preamble of two straw men was added on the basis of information in this chapter. In a second layer a discursus on certain ramifications of a relevant sugya in a later chapter in the tractate was added. In yet a third layer a glossator schooled in the details of the third chapter of Makkot changed and added to what was before him. They represent three differing types of unattributed work, a preamble to Amoraic dicta, a random expansion of an extant sugya and a critical gloss. Yet all of these unattributed layers come from the period of the formation of the Talmud as we know it, for all three are creative workings of material and not simply mechanical transfers of previously edited material.[34]

Certain characteristics are true of all three unattributed layers, and they address the questions I posed at the beginning of this paper. In all three layers the questions and rhetorical development are contrived to present certain information established beforehand in another context. This is far from the live discussions in an intellectual hot house which is the traditional description of the Talmud.

---

[33]Their comments are themselves of great interest, and doubt as to their originality, here, and as to their meaning, has concerned a number of scholars in the past. Compare J. Kaplan, *The Redaction of the Babylonian Talmud* (N.Y., 1933), p. 171, H. Albeck, *Introduction to the Mishna*, p. 276, A. Weiss, *MGWJ* 73, p. 210, n. 1, and *Studies in the Talmud* (Jerusalem 1975), p. 122, n. 137, Z. Frankel, op. cit., p. 226 and 256, and J. Epstein, *Introduction to Tannaitic Literature* (Hebrew) (Jerusalem 1957), pp. 201-202 and n. 24. I cannot here deal with what is quite another subject. It is, however, clear to me that whatever the original meaning of the dicta of Yosef and Ashi/Kahana, and wherever they may originally have been set (I believe them to be original here), they were in place in the tradition before the unattributed sugya writers began their work here.

[34]Such a transfer of a complete edited Talmud segment is to be found here too, in the unattributed segment that begins after the Amoraic comments, which material I have not presented in this paper.

Furthermore, each of the layers is quite limited in its scope, both in terms of what it sets out to do and in terms of the body of material it addresses. These are not, then, either singly or jointly, likely to be remnants of the master lectures delivered at the Babylonian academy, which we can assume delivered themselves of a great deal more virtuosity than is in evidence here. What is in evidence here is a slow, literary growth of the sugya, wherein whoever got hold of it might fiddle here or there based on the interest and information he (or she) possessed. That the grandeur of the Talmud, its lengthy and complex debate, may not be an artifact of deep legal debate so much as an aggregate of generations of glossing with an eye to the literary merits of an ornate Torah, grand because it is complex; that that should be the story behind the formation of this book should perhaps be no surprise, for every generation of its students and teachers was driven by the perceived obligation *lhgyd twrh wlh'dyr*.

Appendix A

B. Shev. 5a

It is taught there: "Removals on the Sabbath are of two types which yield four inside and two types which yield four outside."

What difference is there that here it teaches two types which yield four and nothing more, and there it teaches two types which yield four inside and two types which yield four outside?

1. There which is the primary venue of Sabbath it teaches ur-categories and derivatives, here which is not the primary venue of Sabbath, ur-categories are taught, derivatives are not.

    a. What are the ur-categories?—they are removals. But there are only two cases of removal!

—Two cases of liability and also two of exemption.

    b. But does the Mishnah not teach a parallel to symptoms of affliction? Just as there all are liabilities, so here all must be liabilities!

2. Rather says Rav Pappa: There which is the primary venue of Sabbath both liabilities and exemptions are taught, but here liabilities are taught, exemptions are not.

Appendix B

From B. Shev. 20b-21b

Says R. Idi bar Avin...says R. Johanan: R. Judah says in the name of R. Jose the Galilean: Every negative precept in the Torah, (transgression of) that negative precept actively is punishable by lashes whereas (transgression of) that negative precept through inactivity is not punishable by lashes, except he who swears, swaps (profane property for sacred) and curses his colleague with the (holy) Name.

And R. Abbahu deliberated about it: What sort of false oath is this (wherein transgression through inactivity is punishable)?

If one says (it is) 'I swear I will not eat', but he ate—that is (transgression of) a negative precept actively, but if he said 'I swear I will eat', but he did not eat—does that one receive lashes? It is said: 'I swear I shall eat this loaf today', but the day passed and he did not...

R. Johanan says: He is not lashed because this is a negative precept (transgressed) through inactivity, and (transgression of) a negative precept through inactivity is not punishable by lashes."

And says R. Abbahu: Let it be 'I ate' and 'I did not eat'.

1. How does that differ (Rashi: from the other case of transgression of oaths through inactivity which does not merit lashes)?

—Says Rava: "The Torah expressly included false oath parallel to vain (oath). Just as vain (oath) is about the past, so, too, false (oath) is about the past."

2. R. Jeremiah retorted to R. Abbahu: " 'I swear that I shall not eat this loaf, I swear I shan't eat it', but he ate it—he is only liable for one (sacrifice). This is a rash oath for which one is liable for lashes for intentional transgression, and for a variable sacrifice for unintentional transgression."— 'This is' to exclude what? Is it not intended to exclude 'I ate' and 'I did not eat' from lashes?

—No. ...

It is all according to R. Akiba. The first part does not intend to exclude 'I ate' and 'I did not eat'...but rather to exclude 'I will eat' but he did not eat from receiving lashes.

Chapter Five

Contemporary Talmudic Studies: The Continuing Agenda

Michael L. Chernick
Hebrew Union College

The Revolution in Talmudic Studies

The papers preceding this response are each marked by a charting of new ground by means of careful and detailed analysis of Talmudic material. Those of us engaged in the historical-critical academic study of the Talmud cannot have arrived at this point without those who preceded us. As has been noted by the authors of the studies above, some of the methods we employ and the questions we ask today were already part of the medieval commentators' considerations. They, as has been noted, simply did not generalize these methods and questions to the Talmud as a whole.

The revolution of that generalization took place only within this century. It is to teachers like Julius Kaplan, Hyman Klein, and Abraham Weiss that we owe the academic consensus that the *stamot*, the anonymous Talmudic materials, are a late development in the formation of the Babylonian Talmud. This point of view and the studies[1] which attempted to document and substantiate it placed the entire Talmud before us in a different light. It was no longer to be viewed as a unified whole edited by R. Ashi and Ravina during a certain, single period of time (ca. 425-500 C.E.). Rather, the Talmud was a multi-levelled, stratified document. As such, those who studied it needed a new method for doing so, one which took into account this "old-new" reality of the text.[2] We owe these

---

[1] Julius Kaplan, *The Redaction of the Babylonian Talmud* (New York, 1933); Hyman Klein, *Collected Talmudic Scientific Writings* (Jerusalem, 1979), p. 64ff; Abraham Weiss, *Hithavut ha-Talmud bishlemuto* (New York, 1943); *L'heker ha-Talmud* (New York, 1954); and *'Al ha-Yezirah ha-Sifrutit shel ha-Amoraim* (New York, 1962).

[2] Neither the Talmudic statement about R. Ashi and Ravina being "*sof hora'ah*" (B. B.M. 86a) nor the allusion to R. Ashi's "*mahadurot*" (B. B.B. 157b) truly indicate anything about R. Ashi and Ravina editing or closing the Talmud. See *Epistle of R. Sherira Gaon*, ed. Lewin, p. 93, and the commentary of R. Gershom, B. B.B. 157b. To my knowledge, the first appearance of the idea that R. Ashi and Ravina closed the Talmud is in Ibn Daud's *Sefer Hakabbalah*. See Abraham Weiss, *Hithavut ha-Talmud bishlemuto*, pp. 242-257.

teachers the recognition due pioneers. They not only discovered a new way of viewing the Talmudic text, but they also contributed vastly to the methods we use today to separate stratum from stratum in search of a better comprehension of the text's meaning, genesis, and unfolding.

Today we separate *memra*, the apodictic Amoraic statement, from its matrix of anonymous comment almost as a matter of course. This separation from its surrounding layers of commentary and argumentation lets us look at what the *memra* may have meant on its own. This approach is the heritage left by Klein, who taught us to separate *gemara* from *sebara*; by Abraham Weiss, who distinguished *memra* from *s'tama dig'mara*; and by Weiss-Halivni, whose work proceeds by separating "apodictic Amoraic statements" from "anonymous argumentation." In its way, these moderns can be seen as extending tendencies already present in Maimonides' separation of the Mishnah from its Talmudic overlay, a characteristic of his famous Commentary to the Mishnah. Because of these historical-critical scholars' works, we can discuss the Talmud as literature in a more sophisticated way. We can pinpoint its forms, sources, and clues to development in ways never imagined by the hundreds of generations who lovingly and reverently studied it. In this respect we are a specially privileged generation of Talmudic researchers.

Expanding the Agenda: The Question of the Savoraim

The preceding studies indicate that the work of the "founders" has continued. This continuation is, however, more than a recapitulation of the founders' work or extension of their methods over a larger area of material. Rather, the agenda has become more pointed and defined, and the methodological scope for the work has been broadened.

When Kaplan, Klein, or Weiss said that the anonymous *sugya* was "late," they meant it was Savoraic. The Savoraic period stretches from ca. 500 or 520 until as late as 680 C.E. according to Abraham Weiss. For him, "Savoraic" was as much a description of a literary activity as it was of a group or period. This, along with his particular reading of *The Epistle of R. Sherira Gaon*, accounts for the late date he assigns to the basic end of the period. Until the latter date, and occasionally after it, "Savoraic" activity was the major form of Talmudic creativity. That activity might be summed up in Weiss's own term *shikhlul sifruti*, literary improvement. More clearly stated, the Savoraim interpreted, connected, compared, and "filled in" the sources in their possession. The result was the complex, many-tiered Babylonian *sugya* created by unnamed, but ever-present, continuators of the Talmud.

David Weiss-Halivni has taken the strict chronological meaning of "Savoraic" very seriously. This would reduce its length considerably. He has also accepted the view that there is no conclusive evidence that the Savoraim contributed more than "finishing touches" to the Talmud. Having done this, he has raised the question, at least through the work of some of his more recent students, of when the basic literary form of anonymous Talmudic material, which is argumentation, came into vogue. He has also encouraged a search for the roots of the preservation of the argumentational form. The results have been the work of Richard Kalmin and David Kraemer presented above.

Regarding Kraemer's basic claim of a development of propensity to preserve argumentation in the third and fourth generation of the Amoraim (ca. 280-350 C.E.), I wonder whether such preservation was not merely a rediscovery. Mindful of some of the sources used by him to prove his point, I sought a similar type and form of source in earlier rabbinic literature. At least one such source emerged, and perhaps there are more. The one in question is T. Menahot 8:7:

A. How do they stir them?

B. *"In the case of loaves, they stir [oil into them],"* the words of Rabbi, as it is said, 'Loaves mixed with oil' [Lev. 7:12].

C. And Sages say, "[With] fine flour" [M. Men. 6:3], as it is said, 'Flour mixed with oil [Lev. 7:23].

D. He said to them, "Still is the matter subject to debate. Who shall settle the matter?"

E. They said to him, "Here *loaves* is stated, and in connection with the thank-offering *loaves* is stated. Just as *loaves* stated in connection with the thank-offering [means] that it is not possible to stir them without fine flour, so *loaves* stated in this case [means] that it is not possible to stir them without fine flour."

F. Said Rabbi, "I prefer their opinion to my opinion."*

Here, according to Kraemer's criterion, Rabbi records or preserves his argument with Sages as well as his ultimate agreement with their position. Ch. Albeck and others have categorized passages which include formulas like "Rabbi said, I said..." as collections of the "Talmud" of Rabbi.[3] "Talmud" in this case means the preservation of argument, and would mean that to the Amoraim. Also, argumentative formulations appear with frequency in halakhic midrash

---

*Translation: Jacob Neusner, *The Tosefta. Translated from the Hebrew. Fifth Division: Qodoshim* (New York, 1979), p. 134. (Editor)

[3]H. Albeck, *Mavo la-Mishnah* (Jerusalem-Tel Aviv, 1959), pp. 284-85; J.N. Epstein, *M'vo'ot l'Sifrut ha-Tannaim* (Jerusalem, 1957, 2nd edition, 1979), p. 211.

passages. They are different from the Talmudic *sugya* in a variety of ways already noted by Abraham Weiss.[4] Nevertheless, if such material is early, meaning earlier than the Amoraim in David Kraemer's sources, it may be regarded as a record of preservation of argumentation which precedes the Amoraic period and influences it. It seems to me that these sort of sources are worth finding and researching carefully in the search for the roots of the preservation of argumentation and its centrality in the final form of the Babylonian Talmud.

Beyond these considerations, I feel that some of the sources David Kraemer used to prove his point may not serve his thesis well. I will limit my critique to some examples to which he refers in his notes. He cites as cases of preservation of argumentation passages in B. Ber. 25b and 48a. These passages, though attributed to different Amoraim (Zeira and R. Joseph), share the same basic literary formulation. Rabbah's statements cited in B. Eruv. 40a and 40b are part of literary unit identified by A. Weiss as a *kovez*, a collection of dicta.[5] Its character in this case is a uniform literary pattern for presenting two halakhic rulings about the Rosh Ha-Shanah liturgy.[6]

The fact that the above-mentioned sources have such a highly finished literary form calls Kraemer's dating of preservation of argumentation into question. It is true that the attributions are to third generation Amoraim, but the formulation and publication of the statements are not necessarily contemporaneous with the speakers. Who was responsible for casting these statements in the form we have them? If the tradents themselves, then we would have to posit the known existence of set forms and literary devices already in place, current, and fashionable by their time. This would suggest at least the possibility of an interest in preservation of argumentation prior to the third generation of Amoraim. On the other hand, since all these traditions share the opening formula "'*mr* X," it is most likely that they received their present wording from later "formulators." Thus, we face the possibility that there was no concern for the formal preservation of argumentation except as students' notes—or their oral

---

[4]Abraham Weiss, *'Al ha-Yezirah ha-Sifrutit shel ha-Amoraim*, p. 7.

[5]Ibid., pp. 176-250.

[6]There are three statements of Rabbah in the full "collection". All three begin with the formula, "When we were at the school of R. Huna, we had a question (regarding)...." The last two statements in the "collection" include the additional formula, "...he did not have (the answer) in hand. I came before R. Judah...." The last statement in the "collection" is unrelated to the Rosh Hashanah liturgy issues, but it joins the "collection" due to its shared formula. For a full discussion of this source see Abraham Weiss, *'Al ha-Yezirah ha-Sifrutit shel ha-Amoraim*, pp. 209-210.

equivalent, depending on which theory of transmission one espouses—until a point well beyond Zeira, Joseph, and Rabbah.

Why the issues of literary conventions and formulary similarity were not given more weight in David Kraemer's work is, I believe, an issue which hinges on what I might describe as a contemporary "Houses" debate. I will turn to an analysis of that debate shortly. For now, it is important that we recognize what a refinement of an issue we have in Kraemer's work. This refinement lies in the careful search for beginnings, for the roots of what become the Babylonian Talmud.

The renewed concern over the issue of origins is the beginning of a reassessment of the role of Savoraim in the final redactional stages of the Talmud. While the issue has surfaced most clearly for the school of David Weiss-Halivni, the concern seems to be alive as well in the circles which continue in the footsteps of Abraham Weiss. For example, as a student of Weiss and his successor, Prof. Meyer Feldblum, I was urged to look into the development of certain rabbinic hermeneutical methods. As it turned out, formal and stylistic developments in these methods provided some markers for identifying and dating a *sugya* as late. Yet the marker, "the incomplete *kelal*" in late *kelal uferat ukelal* interpretations, cannot be dated later than the last Amora, Ravina, who is the named figure who accepted "the incomplete *kelal*" as legitimate. This marker is a commonplace in anonymous Talmudic passages. Now we must ask: is its use restricted to contemporaries of Ravina or is this hermeneutical element used beyond Ravina's time? In other words, is it late Amoraic or essentially Savoraic? Is the anonymous *sugya* characteristic of the last Amoraic generation, and of it alone, or does that style continue for a century or more into the Savoraic period? Solid answers to these questions are not known at present. What we do know, which we did not even recognize after the work of the pioneers, is that the roots of the typical anonymous *sugya* are late Amoraic. Richard Kalmin's work shows this using the questions and methods of Weiss-Halivni; and following A. Weiss's methods, Avinoam Cohen's thesis on Mar bar Rav Ashi independently confirms it, though this was not his main objective.[7]

It is clear that the contemporary agenda demands a certain skepticism as to the provenance of the anonymous Talmudic material, just as our predecessors were skeptical about the traditional view of a unified, well-edited Talmud. Reflecting on my sense of the Talmud at the end of my graduate training, I realize that while it was clear that the Talmud had its strata, the "stama" was dealt with as if

---

[7] Avinoam Cohen, *Mar bar Rav Ashi and his Literary Contribution* (Heb., doc. diss., Yeshiva University, 1980).

it were an unvariegated unit. This was so despite the fact that Abraham Weiss's view regarding a long period of Savoraic development did not allow for the "stama" to be the work of any one individual. Nevertheless, the anonymity of the contributors to this stratum gave it the appearance of seamlessness and unity. That is why Avram Reisner's "unpacking" of the B. Shevuot passage is so important and eye-opening. It moves us to a fuller appreciation of the multi-levelled nature of even the anonymous Talmudic material. Now we are bound to test the validity of Reisner's methods and findings. If all is in order, we must then pursue a general method for doing the work he has begun, developing a nomenclature to describe what we find, and providing a chronology of developments to the extent possible. "*Divrei Torah parim v'ravim*" (B. Hagigah 3b). The words of the Torah are fruitful and multiply. This seems to be so presently as it has been in the past.

The Need for Eclecticism

The fact that schools of historical-critical approach have formed is good, but it is a matter of concern as well. It is good insofar as there is now a *dor hemshekh*, a generation of successors and emerging scholars who continue the interest and involvement in the academic study of the Talmud. It is, however, a matter of concern due to the potential schools have for becoming methodologically rigid. The existence of identifiable schools means the institutionalization of points of view and concomitant resistance to important developments outside of one's own circle. I, for one, am glad that cross-fertilization appears to be the norm thus far in the critical-historical study of Talmud. Perhaps the limited number of participants in this work makes sharing inevitable. At any rate, Richard Kalmin's work in its present form is characterized by more caution in its conclusions than its previous recensions. Indeed, he has looked at the sources of the post-Rav Ashi Amoraim with a more sharply critical eye because of the critique and questioning he and his thesis endured at my hands and at the hands of Prof. Shamma Friedman. Both Friedman and I were trained outside of the circle of David Weiss-Halivni. Unchallenged by us in regard to the short period assigned for the development of such a massive literary corpus as the *stam* (427-501 C.E.), Kalmin would perhaps not have raised the question of whether there was significant difference between the stammaitic treatment of Rav Ashi and the "late" Ravina. As Kalmin has written, there should have been some noticeable difference based on chronological distance, but there is not. "Why not?" is a question which extends and sharpens our agenda. Eclecticism has borne some fruit.

To further illustrate the importance of cross-fertilization, the following example should serve well. The notion of a major early 6th century persecution which wiped out the Babylonian rabbinic world is becoming less tenable from the Jewish historian's point of view. Yet, according to Abraham Weiss, that notion explains why the anonymous *sugya* contains more forced interpretations of early rabbinic material. The destruction of the main academies meant, for him, the erosion of learning and, hence, of comprehension of the preserved Tannaitic and Amoraic heritage. If, however, there was no overwhelming catastrophe which destroyed the academies, why would comprehension erode and forced explanations abound?

The rich contributions of David Weiss-Halivni's source critical method present a well-documented alternative explanation for forced interpretations. Namely, if one has a similar, but inexact, "tradition" in place of an original, exact source, one is faced with the choice of a "poor fit" or a "retailoring." According to Halivni, "re-tailoring" became the method of choice for fitting inexact material into the Talmudic discussions and debates. Given this theory, one need not point to radical discontinuity of Jewish learning or its quality to explain forced interpretation. Time and distance from sources erodes formulation. One need not point to catastrophe.

The thrust of the examples I have given is that it is crucial for the various "Houses" of Talmudic research to keep each others' work, methods, and mutual critique in view. Halivni's students, especially David Kraemer, opened my eyes when they refused to allow me to define an anonymous Palestinian Talmudic passage as "Amoraic." It was "stam," anonymous, and nothing more could be said about it without further research. "Stam" means something else in my school, but they were right. Our dealing with Talmudic sources—including the nomenclature we apply-cannot merely be the product of credos, prejudices, and predilections which are "received revelation" from our mentors. We, as they, must look for ourselves. We honor best those who taught us when we chart the poorly mapped or as yet undiscovered as they sought to do.

The Contemporary "Houses" Debate

Having urged continued sharing between the various schools of critical-historical Talmudic research, a note about the differences between the researchers committed to A. Weiss's methods and those committed to David Halivni's approach is in order. Abraham Weiss developed the notion that the Amoraic world was one which flourished in a literary atmosphere.[8] It was a world which preserved traditions by giving them a fixed literary form.[9] Basically, Weiss indicates a preference for the position that these pieces of literature were

---

[8]Abraham Weiss, *L'ḥeker ha-Talmud*, pp. 59-63.

[9]Ibid., pp. 64-66.

preserved and transmitted in writing.[10] On the other hand, Halivni and his students indicate that their sense is that the "apodictic Amoraic statements" were created for memorization and oral transmission. It appears that Halivni's view and that of his students is influenced by Lieberman. In his *Hellenism in Jewish Palestine*, Lieberman included a chapter entitled, "The Publication of the Mishnah" in which he held that publication of sources was accomplished by giving them a fixed, oral formula. This was the case among the Greeks, and this was the case for Mishnaic teachings.

The two different views regarding how traditions were preserved have many different implications for the way a researcher will see and read the Talmud. For example, David Kraemer's work is rooted in one conception of the material; my critique of it is rooted in another, each according to differences over the "deformation" of a "source" into a "tradition" as a cause for forced interpretation. After all, the spoken word is more easily recast than the written dicta of one's sainted teacher, though manuscript variants show that writing is no guarantor of perfect transmission. Halivni's source critical method is more credible in a theoretical frame that accepts oral transmission over written. On the other hand, Kalmin's problem of similar stammaitic approaches to the traditions of Rav Ashi and the "late" Ravina is reduced by a degree if we posit written transmission of traditions. A written text of Rav Ashi's words is less likely to be changed and reshaped, even after a hundred years, than an unwritten communication of them passed orally during that amount of time. This might considerably aid later generations in comprehending what Rav Ashi meant.

For the time being, how material passed from sage to sage and from one generation to the next is wholly a matter of conjecture. We operate with faith propositions based on guesswork in this realm, not facts. More needs to be known about such matters, though it is not clear at this juncture whether more can be known. Yet, given the importance of the issue, guesswork will not do if knowledge can be gotten. Thus, we all stand before the commanding challenge of all our teachers: "*zil, g'mor!*," "Go and learn!"

---

[10]Ibid., pp. 93-97.

Part Two

THE SYSTEMIC INTERPRETATION OF RABBINIC DOCUMENTS

Chapter Six

The Political Economy of Religion: The Case of Jews' Economies and the Economics of Judaism

Jacob Neusner
Brown University

"[Aristotle] will be seen as attacking the problem of man's livelihood with a radicalism of which no later writer on the subject was capable—none has ever penetrated deeper into the material organization of man's life. In effect, he posed, in all its breadth, the question of the place occupied by the economy in society"

Karl Polanyi[1]

The study of political economy for a brief moment, in the beginning of this century, with the work of Weber, Sombart, and others, encompassed the political economy of religion. In this paper I propose to renew the study of the political economy of religion, using Judaism as my exemplary case. Let me explain. Economics from Aristotle to Quesnay and Riqueti, in the eighteenth century, dealt with not the science of wealth but rather "the management of the social household, first the city, then the state."[2] Economics formed a component of the larger sociopolitical order and dealt with the organization and management of the household (*oikos*). The city (*polis*) was conceived as comprising a set of households. Political economy, therefore, presented the theory of the construction of society, the village, town, or city, out of households, a neat and orderly, intensely classical and, of course, utterly fictive conception. One part of that larger political economy confronted issues of the household and its definition as the principal unit of economic production, the market and its function within the larger political structure, and the nature and definition of wealth. In political economics of Judaism, we deal in particular with the economic thought of the initial statement of the Judaism of the dual Torah, recognizing, beginning to end, that that thought forms part of the larger theory

---

[1]"Aristotle Discovers the Economy," in Polanyi et al., eds., *Trade and Market in the Early Empires*, p. 66.

[2]Elizabeth Fox-Genovese, *The Origins of Physiocracy. Economic Revolution and Social Order in Eighteenth-Century France* (Ithaca and London: Cornell University Press), p. 9. See also Karl Polanyi, *The Livelihood of Man*. Edited by Harry W. Pearson (New York, San Francisco and London: Academic Press, 1977), p. 7.

of the life and social existence of "Israel," as the theorists represented by the Mishnah understood that social entity in its political and economic existence in the here and now and also in the model of Heaven. What I mean, therefore, by political economy is the study of how a given religious system makes its overriding statement through its judgments of politics and economics, as much as through theology, myth, ritual, and philosophy.

My proposed mode of analysis therefore treats not the issues of economics broadly construed, e.g., how the framers of the Mishnah understood the difference between a commodity and specie, or how they defined the fundamental unit of production. Nor do I suggest that we ask about facts of economic history at a given point in the history of a religious group, in the case at hand, for instance, about the economy of the Jews in the time of the Mishnah or how the Mishnah reveals economic information or even attitudes. What I want to know is the answer to a different question. It is, specifically, what we learn about a religion, e.g., the Judaism of the dual Torah in its initial statement, when we ask those questions that economics instructs us to ask. So the issue is systemic analysis: I invoke economics as an indicator (and, I would claim, an independent variable) of the character of a system in context. From economics as conceived in antiquity, for instance, we gain perspective on the way in which the framers of the Mishnah appealed, also, to economics in stating their world view and way of life.

What the present perspective teaches is that the Mishnah is a document of political economy, in which the two critical classifications are the village, *polis*, and the household, *oikos*. Since, however, the Mishnah's framers conceived of the world as God's possession and handiwork, theirs was the design of a universe in which God's and humanity's realms flowed together. The result is a distributive economics, familiar from most ancient times onward, but a distributive economics that, in the same system, coexisted with a kind of market-economics.[3] Their statement bears comparison, therefore, to Plato's *Republic* and Aristotle's *Politics* as a utopian program (*Staatsroman*) of a society as a political entity, encompassing, also, its economics; but pertinent to the comparison also is Augustine's conception of a city of God and a city of man. In the Mishnah we find thinkers attempting, in acute detail, to think through how God and humanity form a single *polis* and a single *oikos*, a shared political economy, one village and one household on earth as it is in heaven.[4]

---

[3] I explain this matter in my *Economics of Judaism. The Initial Statement* (in press).

[4] That is why I conceive the more profound inquiry to address the politics of Judaism, as the Mishnah presents that politics: the city of God which is the city

The Mishnah's sages placed economics, both market (for civil transactions) and distributive (for sacred transactions, e.g., with scheduled castes and the temple), in the center of their system, devoting two of their six divisions to it (the first and the fourth, for the distributive and the market economics, respectively), and succeeded in making their statement through economics in a sustained and detailed way far beyond the manner in which Aristotle did. And no one in antiquity came near Aristotle, as I said. It was with remarkable success that the sages of Judaism presented an economics wholly coordinated in a systemic way with a politics. In this proposed kind of study of religion and economics, therefore, we find ourselves on the border between sociology and economics, following how the sociology of economics—and therefore this kind of inquiry concerning religious materials—places us squarely into the middle of discourse on political economy. Compared to the work of Plato and Aristotle, the Mishnah's system presents the single most successful political economy accomplished in antiquity.

What about work on the political economy of Judaism that is already in hand? The economics of Judaism, as the economics of the Jews, is hardly an unexplored field of inquiry.[5] Indeed, any study of pertinent topics, whether of

---

of humanity, unlike the distinct cities conceived by Augustine. The matter is neatly expressed in numerous specific rules. See for example Roger Brooks, *Support for the Poor in the Mishnaic Law of Agriculture: Tractate Peah* (Chico: Scholars Press for Brown Judaic Studies, 1983), p. 49 to M. Peah 1:4-5: "...The Mishnah's framers regard the Land as the exclusive property of God. When Israelite farmers claim it as their own and grow food on it, they must pay for using God's earth. Householders thus must leave a portion of the yield unharvested as *peah* and give this food over to God's chosen representatives, the poor. The underlying theory is that householders are tenant farmers who pay taxes to their landlord, God." In this concrete way the interpenetration of the realms of God and humanity is expressed. That conception of the household and the village made up of households, the *oikos* and the *polis*, yields not only an economics but also a politics. And the politics is the foundation for the economics, as, in my *Economics of Judaism,* I repeatedly observe.

[5]For an introduction to the economic study of Talmudic literature, see Roman A. Ohrenstein, "Economic Thought in Talmudic Literature in the Light of Modern Economics," *The American Journal of Economics and Sociology*, 1968, vol. 27, pp. 185-96, who cites earlier writings on the subject, cf. p. 185, n. 3. Later in this article we shall deal with some of the work that has been done. Ohrenstein's "Economic Self-Interest and Social Progress in Talmudic Literature: A Further Study of Ancient Economic Thought and Its Modern Significance," *American Journal of Economics and Sociology,* 1970, vol. 29, pp. 59-70, typifies the work in hand in that field.

the Jews' economics or of the Jews' own economy, of the Jews in economic life or of the economics of Judaism, takes its place in a long, if somewhat irregular and uneven, line of works on the subject. The most important and best known statement on the economics of Judaism purports to account, by appeal to the economics of Judaism and the economic behavior of Jews, for the origins of modern capitalism. Werner Sombart, *The Jews and Modern Capitalism*,[6] in 1911 set the issues of the economics of Judaism within a racist framework, maintaining that Jews exhibited an aptitude for modern capitalism, and that aptitude derives in part from the Jewish religion, in part from the Jews' national characteristics. Jewish intellectuality, teleological mode of thought, energy, mobility, adaptability, Jews' affinity for liberalism and capitalism—all of these accounted for the role of Jews in the creation of the economics of capitalism, which dominated. Sombart appealed, in particular, to the anthropology of the Jew, maintaining that the Jews comprise a distinct anthropological group. Jewish qualities persist throughout their history: "constancy in the attitude of the Jews to the peoples among whom they dwelt, hatred of the Jews, Jewish elasticity." "The economic activities of the Jew also show a remarkable constancy." Sombart even found the knowledge of economics among the rabbis of the Talmud to be remarkable. In the end Sombart appealed to the fact that the Jews constitute a "Southern people transplanted among Northern peoples." The Jews exhibited a nomadic spirit through their history. Sombart contrasted "the cold North and the warm South," and held that "Jewish characteristics are due to a peculiar environment." So he appealed to what he found to be the correlation between Jewish intellectuality and desert life, Jewish adaptability and nomad life, and wrote about "Jewish energy and their Southern origin," "'Sylvanism' and Feudalism compared with 'Saharaism' and Capitalism," and ended, of course, with the theme of the Jews and money and the Jews and the Ghetto.

The romantic and racist view of the Jews as a single continuing people with innate characteristics which scientific scholarship can identify and explain of course formed the premise for Sombart's particular interest, in the economic characteristics of the Jew and the relationship of this racial traits to the Jews' origin in the desert. While thoroughly discredited, these views have nonetheless generated a long sequence of books on Jews' economic behavior. Today people continue to conceive "Jewish economic history" as a cogent subject that follows not only synchronic and determinate, but also diachronic and indeterminate lines and dimensions. Such books have taken and now take as the generative category

---

[6]The edition I consulted is Werner Sombart, *The Jews and Modern Capitalism*. With a new introduction by Samuel Z. Klausner. Translated by M. Epstein (New Brunswick and London: Transaction Books, 1982).

the Jews' constituting a distinct economy, or their formation of a social unit of internally-consistent economic action and therefore thought, the possibility of describing, analyzing, and interpreting the Jews within the science of economics. But that category and its premise themselves still await definition and demonstration, and these to this day are lacking. Consequently, while a considerable literature on "the Jews' economic history" takes for granted that there is a single, economically cogent group, the Jews, which has had a single ("an") economic history, and which, therefore, forms a distinctive unit of economic action and thought, the foundations for that literature remain somewhat infirm.[7]

The conception of Jews' having an economic history—part of the larger, indeed encompassing, notion that the Jews' have had a single history as a people, one people—has outlived the demise of the racist rendition of the matter by Sombart. But what happens when we take seriously the problems of conception and method that render fictive and merely imposed a diachronic history of the Jews, unitary, harmonious, and continuous, and when we realize that the secondary and derivative conception of a diachronic economics of the Jews is equally dubious? Whether or not it is racist, that unitary conception of the Jews as a single, distinctive, on-going historical entity, a social group forming also a cogent unit of economic action, is surely romantic. Whatever the salubrious ideological consequences, such an economics bypasses every fundamental question of definition and method. If the Jews do not form a distinct economy, then how can we speak of the Jews in particular in an account of economic history? If, moreover, the Jews do not form a distinct component of a larger economy, then what do we learn about economics when we know that (some) Jews do this, others, that? And if Jews in a given place and circumstance constitute a distinct economic unit within a larger economy, then how study Jews' economic action out of the larger economic context which they help define and of which they form a component? The upshot of these question is simple: how shall we address those questions concerning rational action with regard to scarcity that do, after all, draw our attention when we contemplate, among other entities, the social entities that Jews have formed, and now form, in the world?

---

[7] I hasten to state at the outset that Jews' role in diverse economies, so far as that role is distinctive, surely permits us to appeal as an independent variable to the fact that certain economic actors are Jews. But what trait or quality about those actors as Jews explains the distinctive traits of Jews as a group—if any does— requires careful analysis in a comparative framework, e.g., Jews as a distinct component of a variety of economies. None of these entirely valid and intellectually rigorous inquiries is under discussion here.

True, the simple fact that Jews have lived in a variety of political and economic settings has not escaped attention. The further fact that Jews' economies flourish within larger economies, on the one hand, and do not form a single continuum through time, on the other, has found recognition. But these obstacles to describing "Jewish economic history" have not prevented the composition of pictures of Jews' economics and Judaism's economics. One solution is simple. People assemble pictures of traits held to have proved common to Jews in whatever circumstances they conduct their economic activities. These traits are adduced in justification of the description not merely of diverse Jews' economic action, but of "*the* Jews' economic history." The appeal is to a principal distinctive trait, allegedly indicative of Jews and not of others and therefore demonstrative of Jews' forming an economic entity, namely, Jews' "marginality." Whether or not that characterization has received precise definition need not detain us. The impressionistic character of the category, its relative and subjective applicability—these matters need not detain us. But let us grant for the moment that "economic marginality" forms a category subject to investigation and replication. Then we surely notice that other groups have taken a marginal place in society and economics as well. Accordingly, the possibility that Jews' economic action and thought exemplify not their "Jewish" and so their ideological traits but their (allegedly) marginal character has not yet attracted attention.[8] It follows that while some may claim to present the Jews as an example of any "marginal" economic unit, without differentiating the case from the law of marginal economic action in general, others, and they form the larger part of the literature, do not even take the trouble.

But the picture of how such subjects as "Jews in economic life," and "Economic history of the Jews"—both titles of books, cited presently—are treated is hardly complete with these abstract observations. Let me point to how the work has actually been done. This I do in two steps, first dealing with work I believe entirely sound and correct on Jews' economic behavior, then with another, and more common, reading of the topic, a conceptually crude and incompetent one. Studies of Jews as an economic entity or of Jews' economic behavior include work that speaks not of all Jews everywhere and at all times, in the manner of Sombart, but of a particular subset of Jews, in a distinct economic, therefore also political-historical, setting. Such responsible

---

[8]We may ignore the flip and indefensible racism in such odd comparisons as yield the statement, "the overseas Chinese are the Jews of the Orient," and the like. These form no exception to the judgment that the comparative study of supposedly marginal economic entities awaits systematic attention, at least in writing about the Jews.

scholarship establishes as fact, rather than treating as premise, that Jews did form a subset of an economy and did constitute an economic unit. Such entirely correct economics of Jews further examines Jews' economic behavior not as an effect of ideology but as entirely rational within the public rationality of economic action in the face of scarcity. And, finally, such work deals with Jews who as a matter of public policy were treated as a distinct economic unit and subjected to rules applicable only to that one unit, which is ample justification for studying the Jews' economy as a distinct subset of the larger economy at hand. I point out as a model of work on Jews' economic history Arcadius Kahan, *Essays in Jewish Social and Economic History.*[9] Specific to a particular economy, concerned with showing that the Jews formed a distinct economic actor within that economy, Kahan's papers seem to me the model for how economic history is to be done on this subject. As to allegations that ideology intervenes in economic action and therefore explains it, applied to the Jews in the notion that "Judaism" leads to economic action of one sort rather than another, in such wise that, in the absence of that "Judaism," Jews would have acted like everyone else, Kahan's papers prove indifferent.[10] It may prove to be a fact that a Judaism shapes not only attitudes but actions, not only in religion but also in economics. But until proven for a given circumstance, that is not a fact; and unless proven for all contexts, it surely cannot explain Jews' economic behavior.

But Kahan's essay does not form the paramount model of "Jewish economic history;" rather, it defines the exception to the rule. Contrasting to Kahan's formulation of a precise area of study and investigation of that area through ample data are several works exemplary of inappropriate readings of the matter. These works are characterized by faults of method, conception, and execution. As to method, they impute to all Jews everywhere traits demonstrated in a single case. As to conception, they take for granted that sayings attributed to authorities by texts composed long after said authorities lived actually were said by those authorities, and, further, that people did precisely what sages said they should do. As to execution, they display considerable difficulty in composing cogent paragraphs and well-crafted arguments. In all, a work on the economics of Judaism, not on Jews' economic behavior or on an alleged correlation between the economics of Judaism and Jews' economic behavior or economics or

---

[9]Edited by Roger Weiss, with an introduction by Jonathan Frankel (Chicago and London: The University of Chicago Press, 1986).

[10]I refer in particular to "The Impact of Industrialization in Tsarist Russia on the Socioeconomic Conditions of the Jewish Population," in Kahan, op. cit., pp. 1-69.

formation of economies does well to review how these subjects have been handled even by substantial figures of our own time.

One representative example is Salo W. Baron,[11] who claims to know about economic trends among Jews in the second, third, and fourth centuries. As evidence he cites episodic statements of rabbis, as in the following:

> In those days R. Simon ben Laqish coined that portentous homily which, for generations after, was to be quoted in endless variations: "'You shall not cut yourselves,' this means you shall not divide yourselves into separate groups...." Before the battle for ethnic-religious survival, the inner class struggle receded.[12]
>
> Age-old antagonisms, to be sure, did not disappear overnight. The conflict between the scholarly class and "the people of the land" continued for several generations....
>
> Class differences as such likewise receded into the background as the extremes of wealth and poverty were leveled down by the unrelenting pressure of Roman exploitation. Rarely do we now hear descriptions of such reckless display of wealth as characterized the generation of Martha, daughter of Boethos, before the fall of Jerusalem. Even the consciously exaggerated reports of the wealth of the patriarchal house in the days of Judah I fell far short of what we know about the conspicuous consumption of the Herodian court and aristocracy....

It would be difficult to find a better example of over-interpretation of evidence than Baron's concluding sentence of the opening paragraph of this abstract. Not having shown that there was an inner class struggle or even spelled out what he means by class struggle, how he knows the category applies, let alone the evidence for social stratification on which such judgments rest, Baron leaps into his explanation for why the class struggle receded. That is not the only evidence of what can only be regarded as indifference to critical issues characteristic of writing on Jews' economies, but it is probative. The rest of the passage shows how on the basis of no sustained argument whatsoever, Baron invokes a variety of categories of economic history and analysis of his time, e.g., conspicuous consumption, class struggle ("inner" presumably different from "outer"), and on and on.

When discussing economic policies, which draw us closer to the subject of this essay, Baron presents a discussion some may deem fatuous.[13] Precisely how he frames the issues of economic theory will show why:

---

[11] *A Social and Religious History of the Jews. Vol. II. Ancient Times* (New York: Columbia University Press, 1952), pp. 241-260.

[12] Baron, p. 241.

[13] Baron, pp. 251-255.

Economic Policies: Here too we may observe the tremendous influence of Talmudic legislation upon Jewish economy.

The premise that there was (a) Jewish economy, and that Talmudic legislation affected economic action, is simply unsubstantiated. How Baron knows that people did what rabbis said they should, or that Jews formed an economy in which people could make decisions in accord with sages' instructions, he does not say. The premise of all that follows, then, is vacant. More to the point of our interest in matters of economic theory, we turn to Baron's program of discourse on what he has called "policies:"

> The rabbis constantly tried to maintain interclass equilibrium. They did not denounce riches, as some early Christians did, but they emphasized the merely relative value of great fortunes.... The persistent accentuation of collective economic responsibility made the Jewish system of public welfare highly effective. While there was much poverty among the Jews, the community, through its numerous charitable institutions, took more or less adequate care of the needy.
>
> Man's right, as well as duty, to earn a living and his freedom of disposing of property were safeguarded by rabbinic law and ethics only in so far as they did not conflict with the common weal....
>
> Private ownership, too, was hedged with many legal restrictions and moral injunctions in favor of over-all communal control....
>
> Rabbinic law also extended unusual protection to neighbors....
>
> Nor did the individual enjoy complete mastery over testamentary dispositions....
>
> Apart from favoring discriminatory treatment of apostates, who were supposed to be dead to their families, the rabbis evinced great concern for the claims of minor children to support from their fathers' estate....
>
> In a period of economic scarcity social interest demanded also communal control over wasteful practices even with one's own possessions....

How this mélange of this and that—something akin to economic policy, some odd observations on public priority over private interest that sounds suspiciously contemporary (to 1952), counsel about not throwing away bread crumbs—adds up to "economic policies" I cannot say. But the data deserves a still closer scrutiny, since Baron represents the state of economic analysis of Judaism and so exemplifies precisely the problem I propose to solve in a different way. Here is his "man's right" paragraph, complete:

> Man's right, as well as duty, to earn a living and his freedom of disposing of property were safeguarded by rabbinic law and ethics only in so far as they did not conflict with the common weal. Extremists like R. Simon ben Yohai insisted that the biblical injunction, "This book of the law shall not depart out of thy mouth, but thou shalt meditate therein day and night," postulated wholehearted devotion to the study of Torah at the expense of all economic endeavors. But R. Ishmael effectively countered by quoting the equally scriptural blessing, "That thou mayest gather in thy corn and thy wine and

thine oil." Two centuries later, the Babylonian Abbaye, who had started as a poor man and through hard labor and night work in the fields had amassed some wealth, observed tersely, "Many have followed the way of R. Ishmael and succeeded; others did as R. Simeon ben Yohai and failed." Sheer romanticism induced their compeer, R. Judah bar Ila'i, to contend that in olden times people had made the study of the law a full-time occupation, and devoted only little effort to earning a living, and hence had proved successful in both.... R. Simeon ben Yohai himself conceded, however, that day and night meditation had been possible only to a generation living on Mannah or to priestly recipients of heave-offerings.... In practice the rabbis could at best secure, as we shall see, certain economic privileges for a minority of students, relying upon the overwhelming majority of the population to supply society's needs to economically productive work.

From the right to earn a living being limited by the common weal, we jump to study of the Torah as the alternative to productive labor. That move of Baron's I cannot myself claim to interpret. I see no connection between the balance between "freedom of disposing of property" and "conflict with the common weal," on the one side, and "the issue of work as against study," on the other. The rest of the discussion concerns only that latter matter, and the paragraph falls to pieces by the end in a sequence of unconnected sayings joined by a pseudo-narrative ("two centuries later...") and an equally-meretricious pretense of sustained argument ("...himself conceded"), all resting on the belief that the sayings assigned to various sages really were said by them.

This reading by Baron of how "the Jews'" policies and behavior in economics are to be studied should not be set aside as idiosyncratic. The obvious flaws of historical method, the clear limitations in even so simple a matter as the competent construction of a paragraph—these should not obscure the fact that Baron's construction of the Jewish economy and Jewish economic policy is representative and not at all idiosyncratic. The received conception first of all imputes to the Jews a single economic history, which can be traced diachronically. Proof lies in works in both English and Hebrew. Take for example the book entitled, *Economic History of the Jews*, assigned to Salo W. Baron, Arcadius Kahan, and others, edited by Nachum Gross.[14] Baron wrote Chapters One through Seven, Kahan, Eight through Ten, of Part One, "general survey," and the titles of these sequential chapters follow: "the first temple period, exile and restoration, the second temple period, the Talmudic era, the Muslim Middle Ages, medieval Christendom, economic doctrines, the early modern period, the transition period, the modern period." That, I contend, is a program of diachronic economic history. These chapters can have been composed and presented in the sequence before us only if the author assumed that

---

[14]New York: Schocken, 1975.

a single group, with a continuous, linear history, formed also a cogent and distinct economic entity, with its own, continuous, linear, economic history.

"Economic doctrines" as Baron expounds them are amply familiar to us: bits and pieces of this and that. The remainder of the book covers these topics: agriculture, industry, services, and each part is subdivided, e.g., under services: "banking and bankers, brokers, contractors, court Jews, department stores, Jewish autonomous finances, market days and fairs, mintmasters and moneyers, moneylending, peddling, secondhand goods, slave trade, spice trade, stock exchanges." Here again, we may be sure, data on department stores derive from one time and place, those on slave trade, from another. But laid forth sequentially, the chapter-titles indicate a conception of a single unitary and continuous economic history, in which any fact concerning any Jew at any time or place connects with any fact concerning any other Jew at any other time or place, the whole forming a cogent economy. Nor should work in Hebrew be expected to exhibit a more critical definition of what is subject to discourse. The same Nachum Gross edited *Jews in Economic Life. Collected Essays In Memory of Arkadius Kahan (1920-1982).*[15] Here is the portrait of a field, as sequential essays outline that field:

The Economic Activities of the Jews
The Cardinal Elements of the Economy of Palestine during the Herodian Period
The Economy of Jewish Communities in the Golan in the Mishna and Talmud Period
The Itinerant Peddler in Roman Palestine
The German Economy in the 13th-14th Centuries: The Framework and Conditions for the Economic Activity of the Jews
On the Participation of Jewish Businessmen in the Production and Marketing of Salt in Sixteenth Century Poland and Lithuania
Economic Activities of Jews in the Caribbean in Colonial Times
Jewish Guilds in Turkey in the Sixteenth to Nineteenth Centuries

and on and on. Nor do I exaggerate the utter confusion generated by the conception of "the Jews" as an economic entity, continuous from beginning to the present. The juxtaposition of the following two papers seems to me to make the point rather sharply:

Jewish Population and Occupations in Sherifian Morocco
On the Economic Activit[i]es of the Moldavian Jews in the second half of the 18th and the first half of the 19th centuries

There is no need to ask what one thing has to do with the other. We just take for granted that Jews are Jews wherever they lived, whenever they thrived, and

---

[15] Jerusalem: The Zalman Shazar Center for the Furtherance of the Study of Jewish History, 1985.

whatever Jews' occupations were in Sherifian Morocco bears a self-evident relationship to whatever Moldavian Jews did for a living half a world and a whole civilization distant. Having cited the juxtaposition of titles, with justified confidence I simply rest my case.

How then do I propose to proceed? First, let me make explicit what I do not believe forms a valid program of inquiry in economic history. I reject as hopelessly obtuse the diachronic study of what Jews in various times and places have done to make a living, that is, Jews' economies, or Jews' roles in economies. We should have to demonstrate that, on their own, Jews constituted autonomous economic units, for such studies to yield consequential hypotheses. Whether or not at specific points Jews formed cogent economic units, whether or not at other points Jews formed cogent components of economies made up of diverse other ethnic components, whether or not indicative traits of an ethnic character have any bearing at all upon economic analysis, whether or not ideological elements of indicative traits of an ethnic character constitute independent variables in economic action—none of these questions seems to me properly framed when its comes to "the Jews."

If treating "the Jews" as a social and economic entity yields utter confusion, recognizing that, at a given time and place, in a given set of writings, a cogent statement of a Judaic system, consisting of a world view, a way of life, addressed to a distinct and defined social group, an "Israel," did reach expression permits analysis of another sort. It is inquiry into the economic thought of a Judaism. Let me briefly set forth the kind of inquiry that, I believe, will contribute to our understand of the history of economic theory within the setting, also, of Judaism.

Economics forms a critical component of a system of thought intended to design and to describe a social world. No utopian design, such as is given by the Mishnah, a classic *Staatsroman* or political novel in the tradition of Plato's *Republic* and Aristotle's *Politics*, can ignore the material organization of society, and every important system of a social character encompasses issues of the social doctrine for economic life. True, in modern times we are accustomed to view economics as disembedded from the political and social system, the market, for instance, as unrelated to kinship or institutions of culture. But until the eighteenth century, by contrast, economics was understood as a component of the social system, and also a constituent of the cultural context. It follows that those religious systems that propose to prescribe public policy and design a social world will integrate into their systems theories of economic behavior and also accounts of systemically-correct economic policy. But how does a religion make its statement, also, through its economics? That is the question I believe we should answer when we consider the economic theory of a religion.

The Mishnah, the initial statement of the Judaism of the dual Torah, ca. A.D. 200, not only encompasses but also integrates economics within its larger system and makes its statement, also, through the exquisite details of rules and regulations governing the householder, the market, and wealth. In this regard, the authorship of the Mishnah finds a comfortable place within the age in which the Mishnah was framed. For its remarkably successful capacity to make its systemic statement, also, through the concerns of economics, its capacity to accomplish the detailed exegesis of economics within its larger social vision and system—these lack a significant counterpart in the generality of philosophy and theology in ancient times. In theologies of Christianity, for example, we find slight interest in, or use of, theories on the household, markets, and wealth, in the framing of the Christian statement, which bears no judgment that we may identify as a statement upon, or of, political economy. Only when we turn to Aristotle do we find a counterpart to the accomplishment of the authorship of the Mishnah. Indeed, as the Mishnah's authorship's power of the extraordinarily detailed exegesis of economics as a systemic component becomes clear to us, we shall conclude that, among the social theorists of antiquity, the framers of the Mishnah take first place in the sophistication and profundity of their thought within political economy.

Clearly, we must read in the context of thought on economics within the philosophy of the age the economics of Judaism in its initial statement, and that approach to the subject brings us to the single influential figure in economic theory, Aristotle. The power of economics as framed by Aristotle, the only economic theorist of antiquity worthy of the name, was to develop the relationship between the economy to society as a whole[16] And the framers of the Mishnah did precisely that: they incorporated issues of economics, even at a profound theoretical level, into the system of society as a whole, as they proposed to construct society. To paraphrase Polanyi's judgment of Aristotle, the authorship of the Mishnah is to be seen as attacking the problem of man's livelihood within a system of sanctification of a holy people with a radicalism of which no later religious thinkers about utopias were capable. None has ever penetrated deeper into the material organization of man's life under the aspect of God's rule. In effect, they posed, in all its breadth, the question of the critical, indeed definitive place occupied by the economy in society under God's rule.

In proposing the systemic analysis of economic thought within a larger religious context, I mean therefore to open many doors, but to close only one. It is the conception that, to define what "Judaism" (or Christianity, Islam, or some other religion) says about a subject, we merely collect and arrange and so

---

[16]Polanyi, "Aristotle Discovers the Economy," p. 79.

compose into a neat collection defined by the topic at hand all topically-pertinent sayings, from all times and places and documents, hence from all Judaisms and all groups of Jews. But that is very commonly how people proceed, that is, without regard to the always determinative dimension of context, let alone to inner logic and systemic discipline and setting. So they present dissertations on topics generally deemed to be, as in the present instance, those of economics. These dissertations may assemble little more than bits and pieces of uninterpreted data about Jews in the spice trade or in department stores, slave trade or diamonds, and brokerage or junk. But on that basis we know nothing at all about "Jewish economic history," the economics of "Judaism" (whatever in context that can mean), let alone about economic actions characteristic of Jews or normative for Jews—and the reasons therefor. Even rather glib judgments about Jews' economic "marginality" stand for premises scarcely accessible to rational analysis.

It follows that mere hunting and gathering form no model for learning, since even data of the hardest kind require a context or remain mere gibberish. Sayings about the value of work, about agronomics, currency, commerce and the marketplace, correct management of labor—by themselves these too tell us nothing about economics as a theoretical construct and as a component of a still larger construction of a world, and they certainly do not inform us about what people actually did. Only a systematic reading of such sayings in the encompassing context of a full statement on the theory of economics made by a given Judaism in its well-crafted sources and their well-composed and cogent statement supplies the correct setting in which these discrete and episodic sayings gain meaning and yield consequence. Once we ask about economics, we have to discover what *in the system at hand* constituted an aspect of economics, subject to the definition of economics we now deem serviceable, but transcending what, in the system in which we live, within that definition we understand as economics.

In the simple approach I propose, we may learn something about the theory of economics in the system under analysis.[17] We shall learn nothing about economic behavior of Jews, either as individuals or as a group, at any time in their history. Let me make a simple statement about why I do not treat matters of fact—actual economic action, for instance—but focus only upon matters of theory. I simply dismiss as merely primitive any notion that people did, or do, what holy books allege they did or should do. That idle nonsense cannot detain

---

[17]Given the long history of the official, Christian economics, from medieval times forward, I am inclined to see in the proposed renewal of political economy of religion a considerable program indeed. And then there is Islam!

learning any longer. We know only what the holy books, beginning with the Mishnah, said, but not what people actually did and why they did it. So the economic history of Jews in antiquity is accessible only in bits and pieces insufficient to compose an account either of the economics of the Jews of the land of Israel or, all the more so, the economic theory that is palpable in the things they actually did.

It may be of interest to point to further inquiries ahead. Specifically, that the same critique of "Jewish economic history" and "the economics of Judaism" is to be said concerning the "Jews' political behavior" and the politics of Judaism is obvious. But at this time, in general, studies of the politics of Jews in relationship to Judaism present a still more abysmal picture than those on the economics of Judaism and economic action of Jews. Collections of sayings on topics deemed political are published even now as accounts of "Jewish political theory" or "the political theory of Judaism," or even as efforts to explain Jews' political conduct in the past and in the world today. I find stupefying the methodological crudity of these modes of discourse on issues of economics, politics, and philosophy, when it comes to the study of the Jews and of Judaisms. I therefore do not exaggerate the theoretical and methodological state of affairs in saying that my establishing a systemic context, on the one side, and my effort to find out what, within a system, economics was or is, represent radically new approaches.

The world-construction, Judaism, encompasses all subjects addressing an entire nation and society, "Israel," whatever group of Jews in such a world-construction constitutes "Israel." And such a program of world-construction therefore by its nature involves three principal intellectual tasks of theoretical thought. These cover the construction's theoretical statement, as a system, of a theory of politics, economics, and learning. Western civilization, for instance, rests upon the politics of democracy, the economics of capitalism,[18] and the learning of science and technology. What of the Judaic system of the dual Torah? Can we identify its politics, economics, and its modes of philosophical thought and systematic inquiry that form the counterpart to philosophy, including natural philosophy? Answers to that question form the first step in an effort to describe the world-construction, Judaism, in any of its versions ("Judaisms"). Not only so, but even today, both in the State of Israel and elsewhere, important systems of thought claim to set forth (a) Judaism by which groups of Jews may compose and construct their societies, their cultures, their ways of life and world-views—their Judaism. Any claim to address the

---

[18]Of which, I think it is clear, socialism must be regarded as an epiphenomenon of transient consequence.

contemporary world in the name of that Judaism must answer the questions that world-constructions must answer and do answer, and (it goes without saying) statements of the answer must adduce in evidence and argument and syllogism not merely discrete and episodic sayings on this and that ("work hard") but a whole and considered theory of matters ("work hard because God works hard").

There is a still more interesting reason for engaging in the study of the economics, politics, and modes of thought we know as philosophy of a given Judaism. In the interpretation of any religious system, such as the Judaism of the dual Torah, we have to compare what one system sets forth with what other systems present. If we are to interpret the Judaism of the dual Torah consequently, we have to undertake comparison with other modes—competing modes indeed!—of the formation of (a) civilization. These are not only or, today, mainly religious. So far, therefore, as we wish to make sense of one system, we require occasions for comparison with other systems, such as are presented by economics, politics, and modes of thought.[19] But if we are to compare system to system, we have to learn, also, how to compare economics to economics, political economy to political economy, even to know what component of a given system serves as the counterpart and corresponding component to the economics of another system, beginning, of course, with our own. So we address in a very particular framework the question of translating from one culture to another the theory of economics, that is, rational action in regard to scarcity, and, in a subsidiary sense, also to the increase and disposition of wealth. What we wish to know is how we may describe the economics of a world different from our own, and so, ultimately, penetrate into the meaning of rationality, encompassing rational action in matters of scarcity and also wealth, its increase and disposition, in a universe other than the familiar one of the secular West.

To do so, we cannot simply adopt and apply to an alien world that contemporary and commonplace theory of economics that for us describes and accounts for the rationality of economic action. That would tell us nothing about rational economic action in a world in which rationality bears different rules from the ones we know. Rather, we have to identify within that other world, different from our own, the things that to them fell into the category we know as economic. Specifically, we ask, what are the things they deemed rational actions in regard to scarcity, and also to matters of wealth, its increase and disposition? And how did they uncover hypotheses of rationality in economic action and test them and translate them into rules of intelligent

---

[19]I refer to my *The Making of the Mind of Judaism. The Formative Age* (Atlanta: Scholars Press for Brown Judaic Studies, 1988).

economic action? In this way we do not merely adopt, but we adapt the issues of economics by allowing economic action to follow rules different from the ones we know, yet to accord with conceptions we nonetheless can claim to understand. Specifically, when we can answer those questions, we know the economics of that other world, that is, we can translate economics from one world to the other. We are able to ask our questions about economics—theory of rational action in the face of scarcity and in the increase and disposition of wealth—and also discern and understand alien answers to those same questions: our rationality constructing the program of inquiry into their rationality concerning common issues, differently sorted out.

Chapter Seven
Slaves, Israelites and the System of the Mishnah

Paul Virgil McCracken Flesher
Northwestern University

In his article, "Slavery in Plato's Thought," Gregory Vlastos makes an important point about the relationship between a social category's appearing in a text and that text's presentation of its world view. Specifically, he shows that in Plato's systematic writings, the characteristics of slaves, as well as their place in the system's structure, are determined by the same criteria that organize the system as a whole.[1] Although perhaps Vlastos did not realize it at the time, his work bears important implications for the study of any social category in the documents of antiquity. Let me state his claim in a more general form. For any document that forms a product of an ordered system, its constituent elements replicate the whole and the whole replicates its parts. In other words, both the overall system and its constituent elements conform to a single principle or set of principles. This point has significant bearing on our study of the Mishnah's portrayal of slavery, for it indicates the proper context for the analysis of its category of slaves, namely, the governing principles of the system itself. But before we address the Mishnah's depiction of slavery, let us study how Vlastos works out his claim with regard to Plato.

"Plato," according to Vlastos, "thinks of the slave's condition as a deficiency of reason. He has *doxa* but no *logos*. He can have true belief, but cannot know the truth of his belief."[2] This means the slave can possess true knowledge, but he cannot know that he does, for he lacks the power of reason to ascertain the accuracy of his beliefs. Thus, a slave is inherently unstable; without even knowing it he could exchange his correct knowledge for incorrect knowledge. The slave's master, of course, possesses both *doxa* and *logos*; he can both know the truth and know that he knows it. This condition, for Plato, is the requisite characteristic for governing. The master rules his slave because he possesses *logos*. The slave cannot rule anyone because he does not. Thus the household

---

[1]Gregory Vlastos, "Slavery in Plato's Thought," in Moses I. Finley, ed., *Slavery in Classical Antiquity: Views and Controversies* (Cambridge: Heffer, 1960), pp. 133-148. First printed in *The Philosophical Review*, vol. 50, 1941, pp. 289-304.

[2]Vlastos, p. 133.

presents a clear hierarchy. Those with *logos* rule over those who possess only *doxa*.

This hierarchy, Vlastos continues, constitutes a systemic principle for Plato which determines the characteristics and position of the primary elements of his system. On the political level, the ruler of the state stands in the same hierarchical relationship to his subjects. He possesses the *logos* necessary to govern, while the citizens and other people must obey him because they lack such power. Vlastos states:

> ...the absence of self-determination, so striking in the case of the slave, is normal in Platonic society. The fully enlightened aristocrats are a small minority of the whole population. All the rest are in some degree *douloi* [that is, slaves] in Plato's sense of the word: they lack *logos*; they do not know the Good and cannot know their own good or the good of the state; their only chance of doing the good is to obey implicitly the commands of their superiors.
>
> ...In other words, Plato uses one and the same principle to interpret (and justify) political authority and the master's right to govern the slave, political obligation and the slave's duty to obey his master.[3] [Brackets mine]

Vlastos goes on to show that Plato applies this principle at two further levels, the human body and the cosmos. In the body, the soul rules the flesh. This is because the soul takes part in *logos*, while the flesh does not. In the cosmos, Plato likewise posits two levels. The primary cause comprises a divine intelligence—a demiurge if you will—which possesses *logos*. This capacity enables the demiurge to institute order in the universe. Accompanying this primary cause is a secondary one, that of material necessity. Since material lacks *logos*, it is irrational and disorderly. In this way, Plato organizes even the two ultimate cosmic forces according to the criterion of *logos*.

Vlastos concludes that Plato's "views about slavery, state, man and the world, all illustrate a single hierarchic pattern; and that the key to the pattern is in his idea of *logos* .... The slave lacks *logos*; so does the multitude in the state, the body in man and material necessity in the universe."[4] Thus, Vlastos shows that in Plato's thought, the system's organizing principle is replicated in each of its members. The social category of the slave derives its definition from the same systemic principle that organizes the primary elements in the system and therefore the system as a whole.

---

[3]Vlastos, pp. 135-137.
[4]Vlastos, p. 147.

When we turn from Plato's thought to the Mishnah, we discover that Vlastos' claim for slavery in Plato's system also applies to slavery there.[5] That is, the Mishnah's framers formulate their concept of slavery according to the same principles used to organize their overall system. In the Mishnah's case, however, the key is not *logos*, but the power of will. This is clear in two central components of the Mishnah's system, the householder and God—reified by the Temple cult. The place of will in these two components has already been demonstrated by Roger Brooks, Howard Eilberg-Schwartz and others—in particular for purity, sacrifices, and tithes; in the sphere of the householder, for poor support and the evaluation of human action.[6] Although I could spend some time describing the position of will in these schemes, it is more profitable for the purposes of this paper to turn to the Mishnah's social system. There, the concept of will supplies the feature by which the framers divide human beings into the Mishnah's most fundamental categories. The four categories of Israelites—the only human beings that matter in the Mishnah—are householders, slaves, minor sons, and women. Let me take a moment to describe, from a theoretical standpoint, the workings of taxonomy; then I will show how the power of will serves to distinguish these four categories.

Taxonomic classification arranges an internally-undifferentiated collection of items into sub-groups or categories whose members share common features. Logically, this is a two-step process. When confronted with unclassified objects, a person first decides upon the characteristic to be used for classification. This is called the taxonomic criterion. Next, on the basis of this criterion, he separates the objects into different categories. Imagine, for example, a person

---

[5]Although there are important differences between Plato's writings and the Mishnah, they are similar in that they are based upon a system. One is philosophy, the other legal discussions. But they both have a specific organization of the world that they are trying to discuss. Plato, in his *Laws* or in his *Republic*, attempts to state his world view explicitly and systematically. The Mishnah's framers, on the other hand, assume a world view and focus on problematic aspects of it. They do not attempt to state the system whole. The point is that despite the difference in genre, both Plato and the Mishnah's framers based their writings on a systemic construction of the world.

[6]Roger Brooks, *Support for the Poor in the Mishnaic Law of Agriculture: Tractate Peah* (Chico, CA: Scholars Press, 1983), esp. pp. 17-19. Howard Eilberg-Schwartz, *The Human Will in Judaism: The Mishnah's Philosophy of Intention* (Atlanta, GA: Scholars Press, 1986). Martin S. Jaffee, *Mishnah's Theology of Tithing: A Study of Tractate Maaserot* (Chico, CA: Scholars Press, 1981). Alan J. [Avery-]Peck, *The Priestly Gift in Mishnah: A Study of Tractate Terumot* (Chico, CA: Scholars Press, 1981).

who has never seen fruit in his life discovering a bowl of bananas, oranges and peaches. How would he or she classify them? They could choose to use shape as the taxonomic criterion. This would result in two categories, one consisting of the bananas, the other of peaches and oranges, since they both are round. Or, if they differentiated according to taste, they would distinguish three kinds of fruit, since each has a distinct flavor. Thus, the taxonomic criterion chosen determines the items that belong to a category.

Turning back to the Mishnah's classification of people, we find that its framers use different permutations of the power of will as the taxonomic criteria to distinguish each of the four categories of human beings.[7] The extent to which different types of people have the power of will and can use it determines the categories into which they are classified. Let me specify the four classes of people and their taxonomic criterion.

Category one, the householder: The householder constitutes the main category of human beings. He possesses the full capacity of will and can use it without any automatic restriction.[8] He thus sets the standard by which all other human categories in the Mishnah are determined. Indeed, all other categories are delineated in contrast to him.

Category two, the minor son: The Mishnah's authorities distinguish the category of minor son as the opposite of the householder's possession of will. The householder has the power of will, the minor son does not. This is because, in the Mishnah's system, a person's power of will is linked to his maturity. Since the minor son is immature, he has no capacity of will.

Category three, the woman: The Mishnah's general category of women is distinguished by gender. Whereas householders are male, women are differentiated by their sexual difference. At this level, the power of will plays no taxonomic role. However, when we examine the six sub-categories of women, the power of will rises to the fore. As Judith Romney Wegner has demonstrated, the Mishnah's framers divide women into three pairs of categories: minor and adult daughters, wives and divorcees, and levirate widows and "normal" widows.[9] Within each pair, the categories are distinguished by the criterion of will,

[7]The following discussion discussion is based on my book, *Oxen, Women, or Citizens? Slaves in the System of the Mishnah* (Atlanta, GA: Scholars Press, 1988).

[8]See Chapter Six of my book, *Oxen, Women, or Citizens? Slaves in the System of the Mishnah*, for a discussion of the limits placed on the householder.

[9]Judith Romney Wegner, *Chattel or Person? The Status of Women in the Mishnah* (New York: Oxford University Press, 1988). I thank Dr. Wegner for providing me with a pre-publication manuscript of her book.

specifically, by the question of whether a householder controls their will in matters of marriage and sexual activity. Of the first pair, the minor daughter has no power of will and so any transaction requiring this capacity—such as marriage—is performed by her father the householder.[10] By contrast, the adult, unmarried daughter possesses the power of will and her father has no control over it. In the second pair, the wife's will with regard to her sexual activity is controlled by her husband, while the divorcee is free to exercise her own will. For the third pair, the levirate widow's power of will with regard to marriage is controlled by her brother-in-law, while the normal widow's will is her own to control. Thus for the Mishnah's six categories of women, their capacity to exercise their will in sexual matters constitutes the taxonomic criterion for distinguishing them.

Category four, the slave: Like the two previous categories, the sages distinguish the bondman in opposition to the category of householder, this time in terms of the capacity to exercise will. The householder can freely exercise his will, the slave cannot. In fact, the Mishnah's authorities present the slave—or, as I prefer to call him, the bondman—as a person who constitutes an extension of his master's will.[11]   Although the bondman has a will of his own, his master's will overrides it and determines when the bondman's exercise of will is effective. The bondman can thus effectively perform only his master's dictates, not his own inclinations. So, the subjugation of the bondman's will to that of his master constitutes the taxonomic criterion that distinguishes him from the other categories of human beings.

For the Mishnah's social system, therefore, the power of will—arranged in different permutations vis a vis the householder—constitutes the systemic principle that determines the primary feature of each category. There is nothing exceptional about the bondman; he is simply one of the social categories distinguished in this manner. In terms of the systemic principle of taxonomy, he is just like householders, women, and minor sons. Thus, for the Mishnah, the slave is designed according to the same principle that dictates the order of the system as a whole.

---

[10]If we compare the minor daughter to the minor son, we discover an interesting difference. The minor daughter's father can use his will on her behalf (e.g., he can marry her off), but the father of a minor son cannot (e.g., he cannot marry off his son). The difference is gender based; the father can supply the requisite power of will in order to keep control over his daughter's sexuality, but since a father does not control his son's sexuality, he cannot exercise his will in place of the son's.

[11]For a discussion of the categories of slavery in the Mishnah, see my *Oxen, Women, or Citizens? Slaves in the System of the Mishnah* .

We can take this principle beyond the level of classification to the details of the slave's place in the Mishnah's conception of Israelite society. The bondman's subjection to his master's will grants him a particular position in the community. He enjoys a very restricted form of interaction, however, for as an extension of his master's will, he constitutes his master's human tool. We can even compare him to a hammer. When a householder decides to use a hammer for a certain task, he picks up the hammer and uses it. When he completes the task, he puts the hammer away until the next time he needs it. Similarly, a householder decides that a particular task should be done by his bondman and then "uses" him. He informs his slave of the required task and the bondman then performs it. Once the job is completed, the bondman has nothing more to do. Like the hammer, the householder "sets aside" the bondman until the next task.

How does the master's use of his bondman as a tool work in detail? The key to the master's power over his bondman lies in the bondman's will. In the framers' view, the bondman acts at all times with his own will. But the bondman's will is not always effective. The master decides when the bondman's will brings results and when it does not. The householder controls his slave's will as if it were a light switch; he simply turns it on and off. This feature can clearly be seen, for example, when a householder empowers his slave to separate priestly rations from his harvested grain. A householder must separate priestly rations from his harvest and thereby impart sanctity to the designated produce before he or his household can eat it. Neither Scripture nor the Mishnah specifies the amount to be separated, so the householder must choose—using his power of will—the amount to be given. Or, as in M. Terumot 3:4, he can have his slave do it for him:

A. [If a householder] authorized a *ben bayit* [i.e., a free person attached to his household], or his bondman or bondwoman to separate [a specified amount of] priestly rations [from his crop],

B. that which [the individual] separates is [valid] priestly rations.

C. [As regards a case in which the householder] voided [his authorization]—

D. If [the householder] voided [his authorization] before [the individual actually] separated the priestly rations,

E. that which [the individual] separated is not [valid] priestly rations.

F. But if he retracted after [the individual] had separated the priestly rations,

G. that which [the individual] had separated is [valid] priestly rations.

Under his master's authorization, the bondman may validly designate priestly rations from his master's produce. The slave uses his own power of will to accomplish this task, for he must decide how much produce should be given as priestly rations and from what part of the harvested grain it will be taken. His power lasts, however, only for the time in which his master assigns him the duty to perform the separation (A-B, F-G). When the master removes the duty, then the bondman's will has no effect with regard to the designation of priestly rations (C-E). Thus the master's power over his bondman's will is absolute; he can turn his slave's will on or off as he wishes. The Mishnah's framers thus recognize the complete identification of the bondman's will with that of his master.

But the Mishnah's authorities go even further than this. Since the actions performed by both the master's own body and the bondman ultimately stem from the master's decisions of will, the bondman can be likened to his master's body, specifically, his hand. Take the example of a householder who wishes to slaughter a Passover lamb. The householder can decide to slaughter a Passover sacrifice. When he does so, the Temple cult grants full recognition to his action. A bondman by contrast cannot *choose* to slaughter a Passover sacrifice. If a master assigns his slave the task of slaughtering the lamb, however, the slave can then do it. But the cult recognizes the act as effective for the master, not for the bondman. In both instances, then, the householder's will brings about the same result—the cult credits the householder with the sacrifice. By having the master supply the initial will for both, the actions of the bondman become the actions of his master. The framers thus identify the bondman with his master on both mental and physical levels. This identification constitutes the Mishnah's ultimate distinction between slavery and freedom; slavery alters the constituent elements of human freedom—will and action—by sharing some of the bondman's abilities with his master and by depriving the bondman of the rest. By taking over his slave's power of will, the master transforms the bondman into an extension of himself.

Now that we have a clear understanding of how a householder authorizes his bondman's use of will, let us examine how he prevents the slave from using it. To refer to our previous analogy, a householder can use a bondman in the same way he uses a hammer. But when the householder finishes using the hammer, it lies where it was placed, doing nothing. It obviously has no capacity to do anything by itself. The state of slavery imposes upon the bondman a human status equivalent to that of the inert hammer. On the one hand, when the master uses his slave, the slave exercises his will solely to help accomplish the master's goals, as we just observed. On the other hand, when the master does not use the slave, the slave becomes as inert as the hammer. When the bondman is not performing a task for his master, the master's control renders him incapable of using his will to cause legal effects. This is the human equivalent of being inert.

The framers accomplish this restriction by enabling the master to shut off the bondman's will when he wishes. To begin with, the Mishnah's framers strip the bondman of the free capacity to exercise his will; the bondman, like a hammer, thus lacks the ability to "use himself." Sages accomplish this not by denying the bondman's power of will but rather by affirming the master's power over this human characteristic. The case of the bondman's taking a Nazarite vow illustrates this point clearly. The bondman can take the vow to become a Nazarite and the cult treats that vow as effective. But the bondman's master can cancel that vow, rendering it and its effects null and void. In this way, the master deprives his bondman of the capacity to use his power of will without his approval.

The Mishnah's framers extend the bondman's inert status beyond even the hammer's inertia. Anyone can pick a hammer and use it, but a bondman can be used only by his master. No social institution or individual other than a bondman's owner can force the bondman to perform its will.[12] To begin with, the master's control over his slave denies social institutions any power over a bondman's will. The Temple cult provides the clearest example of this. In the Mishnah's system, the Temple cult does not require the bondman to perform any acts of worship that require the power of will. The slave has no assigned role or duties in Temple worship. Although the framers make provision for the bondman to participate in cultic observances if both he and his master so desire, in no case does the cult require the bondman to do so.

The importance of the bondman's will in the cultic arena is further emphasized when we turn from the issue of worship to that of cultic purity. In the Mishnah's system, a person's power of will plays no role in the purity system. Thus, the Temple cult requires the slave—like all other social categories—to participate in that system. He enters a state of impurity, just like other Israelites, and he must purify himself by the same processes that other Israelites use. Since, therefore, the system of cultic purity does not require the exercise of will, the master lacks control over the bondman in this matter. This emphasizes, in a negative manner, the importance of will in the householder's control of the bondman and therefore the centrality of will in determining the characteristics of bondmen.

The householder has even broader control to prevent the interference of individuals with his slave than with institutions. In fact, no individual can require another person's bondman to perform his will. On the one hand, the

---

[12]The only exception to this is the Temple cult with regard to matters of cultic purity, discussed in the next paragraph.

householder's control over his slave deprives the bondman from the capacity to have kinship ties and thereby cuts off the slave from any power that relatives might exercise over him. All relationships prior to enslavement—to spouse, offspring, parents and so on—have been severed. Furthermore, any offspring that a bondman or bondwoman may have while enslaved are likewise not viewed as relations. On the other hand, no individual can acquire temporary control over the will of another man's bondman. For example, if a free man injures his neighbor, he must pay compensation—an act that requires the power of will. But if a bondman injures that same neighbor, he pays nothing. The Mishnah's framers view the master as preventing the bondman's exercise of will and thus denying the capacity and requirement to pay recompense. At no point, therefore, is a master required to relinquish control over his bondman to another person.

The results of our study indicate, then, that the Mishnah's category of slave—the bondman—conforms to the same principle that dictates the Mishnah's categories of humanity, as well as the Mishnah's overall system. Even the details of the slave's attributes and characteristics derive from the master's power over his will. We should not miss the implications of this result. On the one hand, it means that the Mishnah does not retain any identifiably-historical information about the slave. Any passage that may have had its basis in the social reality of the time has been selected and reformulated to reflect the framers' systemic interests. It thus cannot be differentiated from those passages composed by the Mishnah's authorities themselves. On the other hand, these results show that the Mishnah constitutes the product of men with powerful minds, of intellects able to perform this enormous work of synthesis and systematization. The analysis of the Mishnah therefore lies not in the realm of the historian, but of the historian of ideas.

Chapter Eight

The Purpose of the Laws of Diverse-Kinds

Irving J. Mandelbaum
University of Texas at Austin

The biblical laws of diverse-kinds (Lev. 19:19, Dt. 22:9-11), which prohibit the commingling of different classes of plants, animals or fibers, are commonly understood to concern the preservation of the order of Creation.[1] Just as God created all things "according to their kinds" (Gen. 1:11-12, 24-25), so are human beings obligated to maintain these classes and to refrain from creating new ones. This interpretation of the scriptural laws of diverse-kinds appears in early exegetical sources, with rabbinic midrashim among them. At the same time, however, it is not clear whether the rabbis who develop the laws of diverse-kinds (in Mishnah, Tosefta, and Yerushalmi Kilayim) are concerned with the actual state of nature. Do they seek to have the entire physical world correspond to the original structure of Creation, or do they demand only that the part of nature that Israel experiences follow this pattern?

To answer this question one must consider the related issue of whether the rabbis apply the laws of diverse-kinds to gentiles as well as to Jews. For if only Israel is subject to these rules, the rabbis cannot intend to affect the whole of nature. In this paper, therefore, I examine the laws of diverse-kinds that deal specifically with non-Jews. My analysis will show that, with a single exception, the rabbis do not obligate gentiles to observe these rulings. It follows that these authorities are concerned solely that Israel put in order that part of the natural realm that it encounters in its own life. Rather than attempt to reproduce the state of Creation in the whole of the natural world, the rabbis seek to have Israel arrange only a small part of nature. By structuring only that part of the natural world that it experiences, Israel places itself in a perfectly-ordered world before God.

This study consists of two parts. I first survey the biblical exegeses that link the laws of diverse-kinds to Creation, in order to show that these rulings were understood in exegetical sources to concern the whole of the natural world. I then turn to the legal materials (found in Tosefta, and supplemented by a

---

[1] See Mary Douglas, *Purity and Danger* (London: Routledge and Kegan Paul, 1966), p. 53, and J. Soler, "The Dietary Prohibitions of the Hebrews," *The New York Review of Books* 26:10 (June 14, 1979), p. 29.

discussion in Yerushalmi) that consider the question of whether non-Jews are obligated to observe the laws of diverse-kinds. These materials include both a dispute as to whether or not these laws are included among the Noahide laws, and specific rulings that deal with a non-Jew's production of diverse-kinds. This analysis shows that, apart from one minority opinion, the rabbis do not include the laws of diverse-kinds among the Noahide laws, and thus do not obligate gentiles to observe them. Although rabbinic exegetes of Scripture do view the laws of diverse-kinds as a means of preserving the order of the entire natural world, the authorities behind the legal rulings are concerned with Israel's acts of ordering alone.

The interpretation of the biblical laws of diverse-kinds as seeking to preserve the natural order first appears in the works of Philo and Josephus. Philo states, for example, that the prohibition against mixed breeding prevents one from transgressing the laws of nature, and also provides a warning to human beings not to engage in unlawful intercourse, whether with beasts or with humans.[2] The rule forbidding commingling different kinds of seeds serves as a means of preserving the order of nature, "for order is akin to seemliness, and disorder to unseemliness."[3] Some of these rules also express the principle of justice, for it is unjust to pair a strong animal with a weak one, or to demand that the soil support both seeds and vines at the same time.[4] Josephus similarly regards the commingling of seeds as opposing the laws of nature, saying that "Nature delighteth not in the conjunction of things dissimilar."[5] Like Philo, Josephus views the prohibition of mixed breeding as a warning to human beings not to engage in illicit relationships.[6] For both of these scriptural exegetes, therefore, by observing the laws of diverse-kinds one preserves the order and justice that characterize the divinely-created natural world.

Rabbinic exegetes similarly regard the laws of diverse-kinds as implicit in the order of nature. For example, even animals helped bring on the Flood by disobeying the prohibition against mixed breeding, a rule that was held to be implicit in the phrase "according to their kinds" (Gen. 1:25).[7] Another passage cites Gen. 8:19 as proof that these animals were included in the punishment of the Flood, for this verse states that all of the creatures went out of the ark "by

---

[2]The Special Laws 3.46-49, 4.203.

[3]Ibid., 4.210.

[4]Ibid., 4.212-215.

[5]Jewish Antiquities 4.229.

[6]Ibid.

[7]Tanhuma Noah 5, Tanhuma Buber Noah 5, 11.

families," and so excludes "those who were of mixed kinds and those who were castrated," that is, those who either did not belong to proper families or could not produce them.[8] According to these sources, therefore, the prohibition against mixed breeding is implicit in nature itself, and so is to be observed by all of nature. Like Philo and Josephus, rabbinic exegetes derive the laws of diverse-kinds from the order of Creation itself, and so see the aim of these rulings as the protection of this order.

I turn now to the legal materials, in order to determine whether they similarly express the view that the laws of diverse-kinds are universally obligatory. The first question to ask is whether these rules are considered among the Noahide laws, those commandments which apply to gentiles as well as to Jews. T. A.Z. 8(9):4-6J[9] lists the seven Noahide laws as: 1) setting up courts of justice, 2) idolatry, 3) blasphemy, 4) fornication, 5) bloodshed, 6) thievery, and 7) eating a limb from a living beast. Following this catalog, T. A.Z. 8(9):6K-8 (re-lettered for this analysis) presents minority views that suggest other laws for inclusion on this list:

A. R. Hananiah b. Gamaliel says, "[A descendant of Noah is commanded] also concerning blood deriving from a living beast."
B. R. Hidqa says, "Also concerning castration."
C. R. Simeon says, "Also concerning witchcraft."
D. R. Yose says, "The descendants of Noah are subject to warning concerning whatever is stated in the pericope [dealing with witchcraft],
E. "as it is said, 'There shall not be found among you any one who burns his son or his daughter as an offering, any one who practices divination, a soothsayer, or an augur, or a sorcerer, or a charmer, or a medium, or a wizard, or a necromancer' (Dt. 18:10-11).
F. "Is it possible, then, that Scripture has imposed a punishment without imparting a prior warning?
G. "But it provides a warning and afterwards imparts the punishment.
H. "This teaches that it warned them first and then punished them."
I. R. Eleazar says, "Also concerning diverse-kinds."
J. It is permitted for a descendant of Noah to sow seeds [of different kinds] or to wear garments [of wool and linen],
K. [but] it is prohibited to mate [together animals of different kinds] or to graft [a tree of one kind onto a different kind of tree].

An analysis of the literary characteristics of this pericope enables us to isolate the earliest form of this catalog. The list presently consists of five entries, A, B, C, D-H, and I-K. Originally, however, this pericope appears to have

---

[8]Genesis Rabbah 34:8.
[9]The lettering is that of Jacob Neusner, *The Tosefta Translated from the Hebrew. Vol. IV. The Division of Damages* (New York: Ktav, 1981), p. 343.

contained four items, A, B, C, and I, all of which begin with the formula "also concerning...." D-H then glosses and expands C, while J-K glosses and qualifies I. If this analysis is correct, Eleazar's ruling originally stated only that gentiles are subject to the laws of diverse-kinds. Eleazar perhaps makes the point that, like the rules of idolatry and witchcraft, which concern acknowledging the existence and authority of God, the laws of diverse-kinds involve the affirmation of God as Creator of an ordered and good world. This reasoning is explicitly stated at Y. Kil. 1:7 (27b), which cites the phrase "according to their kinds" in support of I-K. In Eleazar's view, then, gentiles as well as Israelites are obligated to maintain the world precisely as God created it.

J-K qualifies Eleazar's ruling by maintaining that gentiles are subject only to certain laws of diverse-kinds. Specifically, gentiles are prohibited only from mixed breeding and grafting, activities which add to the categories of Creation. They are not, however, forbidden from mixing seeds or from wearing garments of wool and linen, actions that do not create new classes but only blur the distinctions between existing ones. J-K perhaps reasons that creating new categories implies a denial of God's unique status as Creator, and so is prohibited universally. Commingling different kinds, however, does not involve a new creation, and so is forbidden to Israel alone. By applying only the former prohibitions to gentiles, J-K may seek to apply Eleazar's reasoning more consistently, ruling that gentiles must observe only the laws of diverse-kinds that imply a recognition of God as Creator. In any event, both I and J-K maintain that at least some of the laws of diverse-kinds do not apply to Israel alone, and that gentiles as well as Israelites are obligated at least to some extent to protect the order of Creation.

It remains to ask why the authorities behind the list of seven Noahide laws at T. A.Z. 8(9):4-6J differ from Eleazar and do not include the laws of diverse-kinds in their catalog. Although Tosefta does not offer an explanation of their view, Y. Kil. 1:7 (27b) presents a dispute in which the Amora Hila may take a similar position. As the following analysis shows, Hila understands the laws of diverse-kinds as affirming God as Creator, but nevertheless does not include them among the Noahide laws:

A. It was taught: Whence [do I know] that they do not graft (1) a tree that does not bear edible fruit upon one that bears edible fruit, (2) nor a tree that bears edible fruit upon another tree that bears edible fruit,

B. one kind [commingled] with another kind, whence [do I know it]?

C. Scripture says, "You shall keep my statutes (*ḥwqwty*). [You shall not let your cattle breed with a different kind; you shall not sow your field with two kinds of seed; nor shall there come upon you a garment of cloth made of two kinds of stuff]" (Lev. 19:19).

D. R. Jonah, R. Leazar in the name of Kahana said, "This is [a teaching] of R. Leazar, [who said that the descendants of Noah are prohibited from mixed grafting], on account of [the exegesis of *ḥwqwty* as] 'the statutes that I enacted for Adam.'"

E. R. Yose in the name of R. Hila said, "[This teaching] accords with all [views], on account of [the exegesis of *ḥwqwty* as 'the statutes that I enacted in my world.'"

A-C[10] discusses the scriptural basis for the rule against mixed grafting, a law that is not stated explicitly in either Lev. 19:19 or Dt. 22:9-11. This law is found to be implied by the statement "You shall keep my statutes," which is understood to include all prohibitions that are not explicitly mentioned in the remainder of Lev. 19:19. At D-E Kahana and Hila discuss whether A-C is to be attributed to Eleazar or to all of the sages. At issue is how A-C understands the word *ḥwqwty* ("my statutes"). According to Kahana, A-C interprets *ḥwqwty* to mean "the statutes that I have already given." A-C must therefore be attributed to Eleazar, who understands the prohibition of mixed grafting to be among "the statutes that I enacted for Adam," that is, a Noahide law.[11] By contrast, according to Hila even sages can stand behind A-C, for they can understand A-C to interpret *ḥwqwty* as "the statutes that I enacted in my world," that is, the laws that God established in nature.[12] While Hila thus links the laws of diverse-kinds to the natural order, he does not derive the obligation to observe these rulings from the "laws" of nature. It does not follow from the fact that nature is ordered that gentiles are commanded to preserve that order. Rather, in Hila's view gentiles are subject only to those laws that are specifically commanded of them. This dispute thus lays out two possible positions concerning the question of who is obligated to observe the laws of diverse-kinds. While Eleazar understands these laws to go back to Adam at Creation, and so to apply to all humanity, Hila considers laws concerning Creation to be no different from other divine commandments, and so to be obligatory upon Israel alone.

Having described these two positions, I now proceed to ask which view stands behind the specific laws dealing with a gentile's production of diverse-

---

[10]A-C is also found in Sifra Qedoshim 4:17.

[11]See Genesis Rabbah 16:6 (and parallels) and B. San. 56b, which state that the Noahide laws were given to Adam. This exegesis appears in support of Eleazar's view at B. San. 60a.

[12]Alternatively, according to the commentator Solomon Serilio, A-C understands *ḥwqwty* to refer to the forms that God "carved" (*ḥqq*) in nature.

kinds. These laws appear in T. Kil. 2:15 and 2:16D-J,[13] which will be considered in turn. T. 2:15B appears to imply that gentiles are prohibited from commingling different kinds. However, as my analysis shows, this ruling need not be interpreted in this manner. T. 2:15 reads as follows:

A. A gentile who grafted a peach[-bud] onto a quince [tree]—
B. even though he is not [himself] permitted to do so,
C. he [an Israelite] takes a shoot from it and plants it in another place.
D. [If a gentile] grafted a spinach beet onto an amaranth—
E. even though the Israelite is not [himself] permitted to do so,
F. he [the Israelite] takes a seed from it and sows it in another place.

A-C concerns the mixed grafting of trees, while D-F discusses a similar act involving herbs. These two parts balance each other, with A and D differing only with regard to the specific case cited, and C and F diverging according to the circumstances of each case ("shoot" vs. "seed"). B and E, however, appear to present a more significant difference, for B reads "*he* is not permitted," while E reads "*an Israelite* is not permitted."[14] If the subject of B is, as it seems to be, the gentile of A, then the difference between B and E accords with T. A.Z. 8(9):8J-K's gloss of Eleazar's rule. For B implies that gentiles are prohibited from grafting together different classes of trees, while E, by mentioning that Israelites are prohibited from such grafts, suggests that gentiles are permitted to graft together herbs of different kinds. B thus could be interpreted to mean that gentiles are obligated to observe the laws of diverse-kinds. However, B is ambiguous, and its subject could be the Israelite of C rather than the gentile of

---

[13]The lettering is that of my "Tosefta Kilayim," in J. Neusner and R. S. Sarason, eds., *The Tosefta Translated from the Hebrew. First Division. Zeraim* (Hoboken: Ktav Publishing House, 1986), pp. 258-259.

[14]These appear to be the correct readings of both B and E. S. Lieberman, *Tosefta Ki-fshutah* (New York: The Jewish Theological Seminary of America, 1955), vol. II, p. 619, on l. 58, cites the editio princeps of Tosefta, and a similar passage at Y. Kil. 1:4 (27a), as reading "Israelite" at B. Lieberman notes that a similar phrase at Y. Orl. 1:2 (61a) also reads "Israelite," but he concludes that the correct reading of the passage is that of Ms. Leiden, which does not contain this word (ibid., n. 53). Lieberman concludes that both Y. Orl. 1:2 (61a) and T. Kil. 2:15B agree with Eleazar's position that the laws of diverse-kinds are included among the Noahide laws. As I argue in what follows, however, it seems more likely that T. 2:15 mentions gentiles because they were known to perform mixed grafts, and that T. 2:15B therefore refers to an Israelite rather than to a gentile. Lieberman (ibid., p. 620, on ll. 59-60) also notes that Ms. Erfurt's reading of E lacks the phrase "Israelite," but he suggests that this reading may be the result of an erroneous correction of E, based on B.

A. Moreover, it is not clear why A-C should mention gentiles at all, for the rule of C would apply even if an Israelite had done the prohibited action.[15]

One may perhaps explain the references to gentiles in A and in D by examining passages in Yerushalmi[16] which also discuss mixed grafts that have been performed by a gentile. Of concern in these instances is not whether the gentile is liable for performing the graft, but only whether the graft would be successful and produce a new species. The gentile appears to be mentioned only because the authors of these rulings evidently assumed that an Israelite would not transgress the prohibition of mixed grafting.[17] T. 2:15 may thus also mention gentiles only because they were considered to hybridize plants and trees on a routine basis. If this interpretation is correct, then T. 2:15B refers to the Israelite of C, and does not imply that gentiles are prohibited from mixed grafting.

T. Kil. 2:16D-J concerns whether one may help someone else grow diverse-kinds. The following analysis shows that at least one rule in the pericope (H-I) implies that gentiles are not obligated to observe the laws of diverse-kinds. T. 2:16D-J reads as follows:

D. They do not work diverse-kinds with an Israelite,
E. but they uproot diverse-kinds with him,
F. because he thereby diminishes the impropriety.
G. They do not work diverse-kinds with a gentile.
H. But [in] the [gentile] towns surrounded [by the Land of Israel], such as Bet Anah, Emah, and its neighbors,
I. they work diverse-kinds with a gentile.
J. Just as diverse-kinds [are prohibited] in the Land [of Israel], so are diverse-kinds prohibited outside of the Land.

This pericope consists of two rules, D and G, which balance one another and are glossed by E-F and H-I (which is glossed in turn by J), respectively. D and G state that one may not help either an Israelite or a gentile grow diverse-kinds, presumably because one may not further the growth of diverse-kinds even in someone else's field. Of present concern is G. This rule presents no reason for its prohibition, and so might be understood to imply that gentiles too are subject to the laws of diverse-kinds. However, H-I qualifies G by maintaining that this rule applies only within the Land of Israel (a ruling that appears to be reversed by J). In this view G prohibits one from helping a gentile grow diverse-kinds

---

[15]See M. Kil. 8:1, which prohibits deriving benefit only from diverse-kinds of the vineyard.

[16]See Y. Kil. 1:4 (27a) and Y. Orl. 1:2 (61a).

[17]See Jehuda Feliks, "Mixed Species," *Encyclopaedia Judaica*, vol. 12, pp. 171-172.

solely because the latter's field lies within the Land of Israel. The laws of diverse-kinds apply according to the location of the field, without regard to who owns it. At least according to H-I, therefore, G presupposes that gentiles are not subject to the laws of growing diverse-kinds.

Now, although H-I would differ with Eleazar, whose rule in its earliest form states that non-Jews are subject to all of the laws of diverse-kinds, it is possible that H-I would agree with the gloss at T. A.Z. 8(9):8J-K, which prohibits gentiles only from mixed grafting and mixed breeding. There is no evidence, however, to suggest that H-I either supports or opposes this view. Moreover, it is possible that T. Kil. 2:16D-J raises the question of the gentile for the same reason that T. 2:15 does. Just as the latter text may discuss a gentile's growing of diverse-kinds solely to ask concerning an Israelite's observance of the law, so T. 2:16D-F may introduce the gentile only to consider the problem of growing diverse-kinds in the Land of Israel. In both instances the gentile may be mentioned only because what he does affects the Israelite, but not because the gentile is also subject to the laws. At the very least, therefore, we may conclude that neither T. 2:15 nor T. 2:16D-G need be interpreted to presuppose Eleazar's view, and that T. 2:16H-I implies the opposing view that gentiles are exempt from observing the laws of diverse-kinds.

Although their views are somewhat ambiguous, it seems likely that the authorities behind the two passages in Tosefta would agree with the majority view, against the opinion of Eleazar, that the laws of diverse-kinds are not included among the Noahide commandments. They would presumably take the position of Hila that even though the categories of plants, animals, and fibers were established at Creation, it does not follow that gentiles are obligated to maintain them. By not applying the laws of diverse-kinds to gentiles, these authorities implicitly maintain that their aim is not to have the entire realm of nature conform to its original state, but only to have Israel order that part of nature that lies within its experience. Of concern is the order of Israel's world, and not that of the world as a whole.

This emphasis on Israel's acts of ordering the natural world fits in well with the larger program presented by the rabbis. This program also calls for ordering, but on a different scale, requiring the placing of all things in their proper categories of either holiness or uncleanness. Jacob Neusner[18] describes this plan in his account of the Judaism of the Mishnah:

> The Mishnah's evidence presents a Judaism which at its foundations and through all of its parts deals with a single fundamental question: What can a

---

[18]*Judaism: The Evidence of Mishnah* (Chicago: The University of Chicago Press, 1981), p. 282.

man do? The evidence of the Mishnah points to a Judaism which answers this question simply: Man, like God, makes the world work. If man wills it, nothing is impossible. When man wills it, all things fall subject to that web of intangible status and incorporeal reality, with a right place for all things, each after its kind, all bearing their proper names, described by the simple word, sanctification. The world is inert and neutral. Man by his word and will initiates the processes which force things to their rightful place on one side or other of the frontier, the definitive category, holiness. That is the substance of the Judaism of the Mishnah.

The goal of the early rabbis, therefore, is to create a perfectly-ordered world. The laws of diverse-kinds form one part of this program by seeking to arrange the natural world in its own categories according to the pattern of Creation. These laws apply only to Israel just as Jews alone have the ability to render all things holy or unclean.[19] And just as these latter categories can apply only to items that lie within Israel's experience, so too can only that part of nature that Israel encounters be properly ordered to correspond with the original order of Creation. The ability to order, and the world that is to be ordered, belong to Israel alone.

We are now in a better position to understand the basis of the dispute between Eleazar and sages concerning the inclusion of the laws of diverse-kinds among the Noahide commandments. Even though he would presumably not accord a gentile's will the ability to effect sanctification or uncleanness, Eleazar does obligate gentiles to order the natural world. Eleazar perhaps reasons that since the categories of this world stem from Creation, and not from laws given specifically to Israel, all people have an obligation to honor them. Eleazar thus aims to have the entire natural world placed in order, while the categories of sacred and unclean still apply only within Israel's experience. By contrast, the majority of sages treats the ordering of the natural world no differently from other acts of ordering (as Hila explains in the Yerushalmi passage cited above), and so subject Israel alone to these laws. In their view, then, the categories of order, whether in the natural world or in the realm of holiness and uncleanness, apply only to what Israel encounters.

The purpose of the laws of diverse-kinds, therefore, is to preserve the order of Creation. This order is to be maintained, however, not in the whole of the natural world, but only in that part that Israel experiences. Israel alone has the power and responsibility to classify all of God's creations according to their kinds, just as it discriminates between the sacred and the unclean. By ordering

---

[19]Although the above-cited passage, for its own purposes, speaks of "men," sages, unless they explicitly state otherwise, always refer specifically to Israel.

its own world, the center and microcosm of God's larger universe, Israel prepares the world as a whole for its Creator's blessing.[20]

---

[20]Earlier versions of this paper were read at the Western Regional Meeting of the National Association for Professors of Hebrew (April 3, 1987), and in the History and Literature of Early Rabbinic Judaism section of the Annual Meeting of AAR-SBL (December 7, 1987). My thanks to the participants in those sessions for their comments. Special thanks to Professor Alan Avery-Peck, Tulane University, for his careful reading of the paper and numerous helpful suggestions. This paper draws in part upon research done under a grant from the Division of Research Programs of the National Endowment for the Humanities. I am grateful to the NEH for its support.

Part Three

EARLY JUDAISM IN ITS GRAECO-ROMAN CONTEXT

Chapter Nine

Shepherds:
Hellenism, Sectarianism, and Judaism

Sandra R. Shimoff
University of Maryland Baltimore County

The Hebrew Scriptures contain many references to shepherding as an honorable occupation. God preferred the offering of the shepherd Abel to that of the farmer Cain. Later, we are introduced to the shepherd-Patriarchs, as well as to Moses, Saul, and David, all of whom were shepherds before serving as leaders of God's flock. The very metaphor of Israel as God's flock attests to the centrality of the image of the shepherd in early biblical literature. The occasional negative characterization of the shepherd[1] is both infrequent and of only passing importance in the biblical narrative. Shepherding was the most common occupation of Israel's early leaders. And the exalted image of the shepherd remained in Israelite literature centuries later;[2] God himself is characterized as a shepherd by both prophet and psalmist.[3]

Given the status of the shepherd in biblical literature, one might predict that rabbinic views would be similarly laudatory; it is easy to imagine the rabbis attributing special Divine approval to individuals choosing the career of the Patriarchs. Aggadic midrashim generally took biblical texts as starting places; as the biblical accounts of shepherds are generally positive, so are those aggadic accounts with biblical bases.[4]

But if the rabbis were willing to glorify the shepherd in the age of the Patriarchs and of the First Commonwealth, they remained adamantly opposed to shepherds of their own age. The statements about shepherds—especially self-employed shepherds—are almost uniformly negative. This study will examine and address this apparent shift in attitude—from praise to opprobrium—in ancient Jewish sources.

---

[1]E.g., Gen. 26:20ff.; Ex. 2:16.

[2]The nomadic life of the ascetic shepherding Rechabites met with Divine approval: see Jeremiah 35.

[3]E.g., Isaiah 40:11, Jeremiah 23:1-3, Ezekiel 34:31, Micah 7:14, Psalms 23, 28:9, 74:1, 77:21, 78:52, 79:13, 80:2, 95:7, 100:3.

[4]E.g., Genesis Rabbah 30:10, 34:3, 97:2; Exodus Rabbah 20:18; Lamentations Rabbah 1:17:52; Midrash Psalms 78:21; Numbers Rabbah 19:13; Ruth Rabbah 5.

The general halakhic stance concerning self-employed shepherds in Eretz Israel is exemplified in the rejection of their testimony[5] and oaths.[6] Rab Judah declared in Rab's name that shepherds in general were incompetent in such matters.[7]

In addition the rabbis cautioned against buying from shepherds fewer than two domesticated animals, two fleeces or two torn pieces of wool.[8] The ruling was based on the explicit assumption that shepherds would limit their thievery to quantities not likely to be noticed by the owners.

The image of the shepherd was sometimes associated with that of the *am ha-aretz*, who also was in general disfavor with the sages. Among the best known biographical accounts in rabbinic literature is that of R. Akiba, who began as an ignorant shepherd and became one of Israel's greatest teachers. Rather than use the story to show how even the lowliest person can attain greatness through Torah study, the story set the stage for rabbinic comments on the crudeness and cruelty of shepherds. In one account R. Akiba is quoted stating: When I was an *am ha-aretz* I said: would that I had a scholar [before me], and I would maul him like an ass.[9]

In a halakhic decision completely at variance with the general rabbinic view of the overriding and all-encompassing respect for human life, the rabbis declared that a Jewish shepherd need not be rescued from a pit.[10] It is difficult to imagine that these are the same rabbis who, in other contexts, agreed that all biblical restrictions may be violated when there is even the possibility of prolonging life.

How are we to account for the extreme and uncharacteristic rabbinic antipathy? Two cogent analyses have focussed on the origins of a particular enactment: the rabbinic decree against raising small cattle in Palestine. Gulak[11] hypothesizes that the regulations date from the end of the Second Commonwealth and represent rabbinic disapproval of the anti-Roman rebels who fled the villages and supported themselves by raising sheep in the forests. The

---

[5]T. San. 5:5 [Zuck. 423], Y. San. 21a; B. San. 25b.

[6]B. B.M. 5b.

[7]B. San. 26a.

[8]B. B.K. 118b.

[9]B. Pes. 49b.

[10]B. San. 57a; B. A.Z. 13b. See also the Soncino edition notes on San. 57a, and T. B.M. 2:32 [Zuck. 375]).

[11]Gulak, A., "*Al ha-ro'im u-megadle b'hema daka,*" (Heb) *Tarbiz,* xii, pp. 181-189.

rebels—and by extension, shepherds in general—were thus viewed by the rabbis as political threats.

Alon[12] has criticized Gulak's hypothesis as both unsubstantiated and unlikely. Instead, Alon suggests that the halakhic position against raising sheep "is no older than the time of Rabban Gamaliel, and that it came into being for perfectly understandable socio-economic reasons. Flocks of sheep and goats were certain to damage crops in the fields and orchards as well as grain, vegetables and fruit-trees. This had become a particularly sensitive matter after the Destruction, because the war had wrought great havoc throughout the countryside, most especially to trees. There was thus a crying need to protect all growing things, particularly those that the country needed most. Furthermore, much land had been laid waste during the fighting, and the easiest thing to do was to use it as pasture. Many husbandmen who had fled from the war probably returned to find their farms ruined, and turned to grazing as the course of less resistance. We may therefore regard this halakha as an inducement to stay in agriculture, which the Tannaim looked upon as the mainstay of the national economy. The Tosefta reads: No man has the right to sell his ancestral holding...so that he may use the proceeds to go into raising small cattle" (T. Arakh. 5:6 [Zuck. 549]).[13]

Alon further argues that the rabbinic condemnation of shepherds represented an explicit long-term economic plan to divert resources to agriculture. Raising small cattle was highly profitable,[14] but could only be carried out at the expense of agriculture. He admits, however, that although his suggestion is internally consistent and possible, it cannot be bolstered by textual citation as none exists: "our sources speak only of the damage which the animals cause to crops."[15]

There are two questions raised by Alon's "economic" analysis: (a) why did the rabbis limit their attack to the shepherd, and generally exclude the owner of the flocks, and (b) would the rabbis have enacted such Draconian regulations for economic reasons?

Why did the rabbis limit their attack to the shepherd and explicitly exclude the owners of the flocks? If rabbinic condemnation was motivated by economic reasons, why did they not condemn the owners as well? To suggest that the rabbis hesitated out of fear of offending R. Judah ha-Nasi (who owned extensive flocks)[16] is entirely unsatisfactory for two reasons. First, they might have

---

[12]Alon, G., *The Jews in Their Land in the Talmudic Age*, vol. 1, ed. Gershon Levi, (Hebrew University: Jerusalem, 1980), pp. 280-287.

[13]Ibid., pp. 282-283.

[14]B. Hul. 84b.

[15]Alon, op. cit., p. 284.

[16]See Genesis Rabbah 20:6.

resorted to subtle devices as adopted in aggadic contexts to criticize the Patriarch and Exilarch.[17] Second, and even more significant, the argument can be easily turned around: if raising sheep represented such a clear and present economic threat, it is difficult to imagine R. Judah ha-Nasi not divesting himself of all such interests.

More seriously, why did the rabbis attack shepherds with such vehemence? The ban against raising small cattle was not a solitary enactment; it was one of several rulings against shepherds and animal husbandry.[18] Alon admits that the ban against raising small cattle "no doubt was observed almost exclusively by the very pious."[19] Presumably, the rabbis were sensitive enough to know whether a halakha was so burdensome that it could not be observed; such enactments were unacceptable in rabbinic jurisprudence.[20] Why would they have enacted a regulation that most of the people would certainly ignore? To bolster a principle perhaps, but certainly not for Alon's suggested economic reasons.

Alon's economic argument thus appears almost as problematic as Gulak's political analysis, and we are left with the question: why did the rabbis condemn shepherds so thoroughly and with such vehemence? No other occupational group has been so singled out. Why were shepherds so often singled out as *ammei ha-aretz*, as of low repute and as opponents of the sages?[21] Why are there no accounts or anecdotes concerning wise shepherds of the rabbinic era in rabbinic literature?

A clue to this enigma may be found in the attitude of the sages to the hellenistic lifestyle that was evident in Eretz Israel during the rabbinic era. The indelible presence of Greek culture in Eretz Israel has been well documented.[22] What had started as casual and culturally-neutral trade relations developed, upon

---

[17]E.g., Büchler, A., "The Conspiracy of R. Nathan and R. Meir against the Patriarch Rabban Simeon b. Gamaliel," in I. Brodie and J. Rabbinowitz, eds., *Studies in Jewish History* (Oxford University: London, 1956).

[18]M. B.K. 7:7, T. B.K. 8:10 (Zuck. 362), B. B.K. 79b, T. B.K. 2:16 (Zuck. 102), T. B.K. 8:12 (Zuck. 362).

[19]Alon, G., op. cit., p. 284, possibly based on T. B.K. 8:13 (Zuck. 362); B. B.K. 80a.

[20]B. A.Z. 36a, Y. A.Z. 2:9, 41d, Y. Shab 1:4.

[21]B. Pes. 49b, B. Yeb. 16a, B. Ket. 62b-63a, Ecclesiastes Rabbah 3:81.

[22]Hadas, M., *Hellenistic Culture* (Columbia University: NY, 1959), pp. 45-46. Tcherikover, V., *Hellenistic Civilization and the Jews* (Jewish Publication Society: NY, 1959), pp. 203 and 346. Eddy, S., *The King Is Dead* (Univ. of Nebraska; Lincoln, 1961), pp. 198-199. Hengel, M., *Judaism and Hellenism* (Fortress Press: Philadelphia, 1973). Stone, M., *Scriptures, Sects and Visions,* (Fortress Press: Philadelphia,1980).

Greek occupation of Palestine, into a clash of cultures. Greek cities were founded in Palestine, complete with Greek names.[23] The example of Alexandrian Jewry was an ever-present reminder of what could follow from unfettered hellenization. There were hellenized Jews in Palestine who resorted to epispasm in order to imitate the Greeks in the Gymnasia, and participated in the Greek games.[24]

Assimilation was rampant, and at least one functioning synagogue used for public prayer was decorated with statuary.[25] There are mosaics depicting the signs of the zodiac and Helios driving his *quadriga* across the heavens.[26] One of the rabbis was known to have bathed with a statue of Aphrodite in plain view.[27] Hellenization was not confined to the Greek cities but also was rife in the holy city of Jerusalem itself.[28]

The upper classes were particularly attracted to the hellenistic lifestyle, but the entire population was influenced; there is much evidence that Greek culture extended to realia. Work and domestic implements,[29] articles of clothing,[30] terms used by merchants,[31] even personal names[32] and hair styles,[33] often reflect Greek contact.

The rabbis themselves were not immune to hellenistic influences; they were, in fact, particularly likely to be exposed to Greek culture. Some served as political representatives of the Jewish community, and thus had to know Greek

---

[23]Hengel, op. cit., p. 14 ff.

[24]I Macc. 1:15, Jubilees 15:13f. Cf. Hengel, op. cit., pp. 74 and 289.

[25]B. R.H. 24b. Cf. Urbach, E. E., "The Rabbinic Laws of Idolatry in the Second and Third Centuries in the Light of Archeological and Historical Facts," *Israel Exploration Journal*, 1959, 9, pp. 149-165.

[26]*Encyclopedia Judaica*, v. 7, s.v. Hammath, p .1243.

[27]B. A.Z. 44b.

[28]Hengel, op. cit., pp. 50 and 56; Eddy, op. cit., pp. 207-209; Hadas, op. cit., p. 31.

[29]Y. Peah 1:1, 5c.

[30]Genesis Rabbah 74:15. See Shimoff, S., "Hellenization Among the Rabbis: Some Evidence from Early Aggadot concerning David and Solomon," *Journal for the Study of Judaism*, 1987, pp. 168-187.

[31]Schürer, E., *Geschichte des judischen Volkes im Zeitalter Jesus Christi*, vol. 2, pp 59-84. Krauss, S., *Griechische und Lateinische Lehnwörter in Talmud, Midrasch und Targum* (Berlin,1898), vol. 2, pp. 623ff. Hengel, op. cit., p. 61.

[32]Hengel, ibid.

[33]B. B.K. 83a. Deuteronomy Rabbah 2.

language.[34] Many Greek terms eventually entered into the text of the Talmud.[35] Rabban Simeon ben Gamaliel offered: "There were a thousand young men in my father's house, 500 of them studied the Law, while the other 500 studied Greek wisdom."[36] There were some rabbis such as R. Abbahu who debated with sectarians,[37] and permitted women to study Greek.[38] R. Meir was renowned for his facility with fox fables,[39] a form of expression popular among the Greeks. The rabbis and sages were not isolationists; their familiarity with modes of paganism is reflected in halakha involving idolatry.[40] They knew even how Roman royalty and their sympathizers lived; what they wore,[41] what they ate,[42] and how they amused themselves.[43] They knew about how emperors and generals disported themselves and how the ordinary and low born occupied their time.[44]

What might the rabbis have heard about shepherds? Shepherds occupied a central roles in Greek mythological themes.[45] The shepherd Pan was god of flocks and shepherds, woods and fields. Apollo, as a punishment for angering Jupiter, had to serve as a shepherd for Admetis. Paris, another popular figure in Greek mythology, was described as a beautiful shepherd. Hellenistic poetry also ennobled the occupation of shepherd.[46] The image of the Greek and Roman shepherd in mythology and poetry would scarcely have met with the approval of the rabbis and sages who would have considered their exploits and antics

---

[34]T. Sotah 15:8, B. Hag. 5b, B. San. 90b.

[35]Krauss, op. cit., v. 2, pp. 623ff. Lieberman, S., *Hellenism in Jewish Palestine* (Jewish Theological Seminary: NY, 1950), p. 3. The Greek author Homer is specifically mentioned by the rabbis: see Lieberman, pp. 105-105.

[36]B. Sot. 49b, B. B.K. 83a. See also Lieberman, op. cit., p. 104, n. 33.

[37]B. A.Z. 4a, Exodus Rabbah 29:5, Y. Taan. 2.1.

[38]Y. Peah 1:1, Y. Shab. 6:1.

[39]B. San. 38b-39a.

[40]Lieberman, op. cit., pp. 115-152. Lieberman contends that the rabbis did not engage in polemics against idolatry, which was not seen by them as a threat to the Jewish community. The present argument does not conflict with Lieberman's analysis; it suggests that the rabbis were responding to Hellenization as a cultural rather than purely religious threat.

[41]See note 30. Cf. Exodus Rabbah 45:2 and 51:8. Tan B. 2:99 and 4:76.

[42]B. A.Z. 11a, B. Ber. 57b.

[43]Eddy, op. cit., p. 244.

[44]B. A.Z. 22a-b. Cf. note to this text in the Soncino edition, p. 113.

[45]Bell, Robert E., *Dictionary of Classical Mythology Symbols, Attributes and Associations* (ABC-Clio: Santa Barbara, 1982).

[46]Theocritus; ed. and trans. by A.S. Gow (Cambridge U. Press, 1952), p. xxix.

deplorable, their display of immorality, unacceptable and scandalous. Much hellenization might have been inevitable, but it is easy to imagine the rabbinic condemnation of the Greek image of the antics and frolics of shepherd-gods—and how such condemnation might extend to blanket denigration of shepherds in the rabbinic midrashic and halakhic literature.

There was yet another reason for the rabbis to discourage shepherding among the Jews. The Romans—based on an account by Manetho[47]—viewed the Jews as descendants of shepherds. Manetho described in great detail how the Hyksos-shepherds first ruled Egypt. The kings of Thebaid and the others in Egypt revolted against the Shepherds; a ruler arose who defeated the Shepherds and drove them out of Egypt into a small area which the Shepherds enclosed in order to safeguard their possessions. Thummosis attempted to force their surrender but could not. In desperation he concluded a treaty with them offering them safe passage out of Egypt. The Shepherds, on these assurances, left Egypt and traveled via the desert into Syria. These people, he relates, founded the city of Jerusalem in Judaea. Politically, this account clearly depicts the Jews as imperialistic. The situation in Palestine just before or just after the Destruction was volatile. The rabbis—at least those sensitive to the repercussions if Romans viewed the Jews as political and occupational descendants of the Hyksos-shepherds—would have done everything possible to discourage Jews from choosing shepherding as a career.[48]

Did Jews of that era know that their Greek contemporaries found the image of the shepherd attractive? We have only to turn to Josephus, presenting biblical account to Rome for Roman consumption. He extols Abel as having been truly righteous and a shepherd, taking only what grew of its own accord; Cain, on the other hand, was a farmer, and farming involved forcing the land and despoiling it.

Thus, one reason for rabbinic condemnation of shepherds may have been a reaction to the hellenistic image of the shepherd that combined idolatry and immorality. But there may have been yet another set of events that forced the rabbis' hands: the prominence of sectarian groups.

The sages and rabbis were always on their guard lest sectarian beliefs become inextricably enmeshed within Jewish tradition. Perhaps the most striking example of sectarian interest in shepherds is to be found in 1 Enoch, dating from

---

[47]Manetho, a third century Heliopolis priest, was the first Egyptian to write an Egyptian history in Greek; Josephus used an abbreviated version on Manetho's work. See Stern, M., *Greek and Latin Authors on Jews and Judaism* (Israel Academy of Sciences and Humanities: Jerusalem, 1976), vol. 1, pp. 62-85.

[48]Josephus, *Antiquities of the Jews*, Book 1. 2,1. H. Thackeray (tr.), (Harvard University: Cambridge, 1932).

second century B.C.E. to first century C.E. The account describes the disasters and predations that systematically decimate a flock of sheep, often a consequence of the sheep's (Israel's) misdeeds. The rulers into whose custodianship they fall are depicted as shepherds. In the end, the Lord of the sheep helps them rebuild a great Tower for worship, and all the other animals and birds pay homage.

This account is a transparent vehicle for the retelling of Jewish history through the eyes of an author who felt that the ritual at the second Temple had been marred through impurity and pollution caused by some of the people. E. Isaac suggests that this work originated in Judea and was in use at Qumran.[49] Essene influence can be deduced from the repeated insistence of the author upon mentioning the white apparel (a noted feature of Qumran dress),[50] as well as the denigrating references (e.g., "blind sheep") to those in control of the Temple ritual. The Qumran sect also objected to the Temple ritual as having been performed in impurity, and held themselves aloof from the Temple, retiring instead to the Judean desert.[51] Once the sectarians had so blatantly co-opted the image of the shepherd, it would be entirely inappropriate for rabbinic homilies.

It has been suggested that Hekhalot literature had its roots in the sectarian circles such as the Dead Sea[52] Sect. This literature furnishes additional examples concerning the use of the image of the shepherd. It is obvious that the image of the shepherd was one of an important leader.[53] In addition, David, who served as a shepherd in his youth, figures as a key figure in some visions.[54]

The role of the shepherd also found its place in nascent Christian literature. The shepherd is consistently presented in a positive light throughout the New Testament. In the Gospel of John,[55] Jesus says that he is the Good Shepherd who knows his sheep; the metaphor of the sheep and shepherd is a recurrent theme in the description of Jesus' resurrection,[56] and remained important in the early Christian community.[57] In I Clement, a work apparently read in the

---

[49]Charlesworth, J. M., *The Old Testament Pseudepigrapha* (Doubleday: Garden City, 1983), v. 1, p. 8.

[50]E.g., 71:1

[51]Vermes, G., *The Dead Sea Scrolls in English* (Penguin: Baltimore, 1972), p. 16. Gaster, T., *The Dead Sea Scriptures* (Anchor: NY, 1976), p. 9.

[52]Scholem, G., *Major Trends in Jewish Mysticism* (Schocken: NY, 1965), p. 43.

[53]Schäfer, P., *Synopse zur Hekhalot-Literatur* (J.C.B. Mohr: Tübingen, 1981), p. 31. Shepherds are placed fourth on the list.

[54]Ibid., pp. 60-63.

[55]10:11 and 10:14.

[56]Matthew 26:31-32; Mark 14:27-28.

[57]In Ephesians 4:11, the term ποιμένας refers to congregational leaders.

assemblies of the primitive church, it is apparent that Jesus was well known in the role of shepherd of his flock.[58] In general, the model of the shepherd was frequently used for didactic purposes in this literature.[59]   Danielou,[60] commenting on Hermas' The Shepherd, states that the oldest segments of this material go back to the year 90. He accounts for the many Jewish features of this work by citing Audet,[61] who recognizes this as the work of a converted Essene. Danielou concurs with this and sees similarities in details in the Dead Sea Scrolls and The Shepherd.

Thus, it appears likely that the extreme rabbinic position against shepherds was dictated by neither ecological nor political pressures, but by much more worrisome threats: Rome from without and sectarianism from within. Were the threat ecological, as Alon has suggested, rabbinic enactments would have been more systematic and broad, rather than focussing on the shepherd alone. Were the threat political, as Gulak has suggested, there would be more internal corroborating evidence.   Instead, the threat was to religious identity, and the sages responded with all the power they could muster.   The issue was so important that it had to be addressed directly; the circumlocutions, metaphors, and allegories of aggada were weapons far too subtle for the battle against paganism and sectarianism. (In fact, the role of the shepherd was so thoroughly embedded in aggada, it could hardly be extirpated; the only hint one may glean is that the role of the shepherd is not excessively glorified in aggada.) The rabbis directed their halakhic weapon against not only explicit paganism and sectarianism, but even against those economic pursuits glorified by paganism and sectarianism—the shepherd.

---

[58]I Clement 18:1, 19:18, 23:17.

[59]Consider III Hermas, Similitude VI:7 ff and Similitude VIII.

[60]Danielou, J., *The Dead Sea Scrolls and Primitive Christianity*, tr. S. Attanasio, (Helicon: Baltimore, 1958), p. 125.

[61]"Affinités litteraires et doctrinales du Manuel de discipline," *Revue Biblique* 60, 1953, pp. 41-82.

Chapter Ten
Chrestus: Christus?

Dixon Slingerland
Hiram College

It is hard to imagine at first glance why a single, perhaps obscure sentence in an ancient historian should evoke so much scholarly interest. In fact, of course, it is not a surprise at all that Suetonius' reference in his *Claudius* 25.4 has assumed such significant proportions, for this one line, "Iudaeos impulsore Chresto assidue tumultuantes Roma expulit," has potential to shed light on many subjects concerning which there is little or no other information available elsewhere. Before the text can be expected to provide much of a yield, however, several basic questions are in need of resolution.

Specifically, who is Chrestus? It has been proposed that this refers to Christianity,[1] to the preaching of the gospel concerning Jesus,[2] to an apostle of Jesus named Chrestus,[3] that it means Jesus who somehow survived the cross and sneaked off to Rome,[4] that it refers to some other Jewish messianic pretender either known, in this case, Simon Magus,[5] or unknown,[6] or to a Jewish zealot[7]

[1] F. Huidekoper, *Judaism at Rome: B.C. 76 to A.D. 140* (3rd ed.; New York: James Miller, 1880), p. 229; H. Janne, "Impulsore Chresto," *Annuaire de l'Institut de philologie et d'histoire orientales* 2 (1934), p. 546.

[2] Among others, H. Vogelstein and P. Rieger, *Geschichte der Juden in Rom* (2 vols.; Berlin: Mayer und Müller, 1896), vol. 1, p. 19; E. Meyer, *Ursprung und Anfänge des Christentums* (3 vols.; Stuttgart: J.G. Cotta'sche Buchhandlung, 1923), vol. 3, p. 463-4; E.M. Smallwood, *The Jews under Roman Rule from Pompey to Diocletian: A Study in Political Relations* (2nd ed.; Leiden: E.J. Brill, 1981), p. 211.

[3] H. Graetz, *History of the Jews* (6 vols.; Philadelphia: Jewish Publication Society of America, 1893), vol. 2, pp. 202 and 231.

[4] R. Graves and J. Podro, *Jesus in Rome: A Historical Conjecture* (London: Cassell and Company, 1957), p. 42.

[5] So especially R. Eisler, Ἰησοῦς Βασιλεὺς οὐ Βασιλεύσας (2 vols.; Heidelberg: Carl Winters Universitätsbuchhandlung, 1929), vol. 1, p. 133 (n. 1), vol. 2, pp. 701 and 706.

[6] M. Borg, "A New Context for Romans XIII," *New Testament Studies* 19 (1972-73), pp. 211-12.

[7] S. Benko, "The Edict of Claudius of A.D. 49 and the Instigator Chrestus," *TZ* 25 (1969), p. 413.

or to some other Jewish troublemaker.[8] Again, who are the Iudaei? Does this mean the entire Jewish population of Rome? Does it refer only to the Jewish leadership? Does it mean just the members of a single Roman synagogue? Is it just the troublemakers? Does it include Jewish Christians? Does it really mean Christians causing disturbances in the synagogues?

And what happened? Are Suetonius and Acts 18:2-3 correct that there was an actual expulsion? Is Dio[9] perhaps better in claiming that Jewish religious establishments were simply closed down? Or, were there two separate punishments of Roman Jews under Claudius, one corresponding to Dio's description and the other to what Suetonius wrote? When did these things occur? Dio apparently dated his event to 41 C.E. Suetonius provided no date, but Orosius[10] claimed 49 C.E. for the material in Suetonius. And finally, why did Chrestus instigate?

Hence, many questions need to be resolved here before much of a yield from the Chrestus passage can be expected. In fact, however, things are not quite so chaotic as first appears. Namely, one important "who" question is easily answered: it was the Emperor Claudius involved in these events. Also, under any circumstances, whatever happened was punitive. It occurred in Rome and affected people in all sources[11] identified as Jews. Thus, this information alone, a punitive action of the Emperor Claudius (41 and 54 C.E.) against Jews in Rome, makes clear that this is a topic both worthy and capable of further study and one, contrary to G. Bornkamm,[12] hardly deserving of relegation to obscurity.

The final question, therefore, concerns the place where this further study should begin. Basically, because an apparently substantial structure already stands on the proposed work site in Suetonius, the first step in the present process is one of demolition. To be precise, among scholars who have expressed views concerning the Chrestus passage, there exists a consensus that the event described in *Claudius* 25.4 marks the impact of Christianity upon Rome. The origins of this Chrestus-Christus identification can be traced to the fifth century Christian historian and friend of Augustine, Orosius.[13] It is not at all certain, however, that he ought to be trusted in these matters, for, following in the

---

[8]F. Blass, "Χρηστιανοί-Χριστιανοί," *Hermes* 30 (1895), p. 468.

[9]Dio Cassius 60.6.6.

[10]Paulus Orosius Historiarum 7.6.

[11]Besides Suetonius, Acts, Dio Cassius and Orosius mentioned above, these include Eusebius *Hist. eccl.* 2.18.9 and perhaps Juvenal *Scholia* 4.117.

[12]G. Bornkamm, *Paul* (New York: Harper and Row, 1971), p. 69.

[13]See n. 10.

footsteps of Eusebius who made the Jewish proselyte Flavia Domitilla[14] into a witness for Christianity,[15] Orosius christianized the persecution of Roman Jews under Tiberius[16] and claimed the famous Jewess Helena of Adiabene[17] for Christianity.[18] Thus, when his interpretation of the Chrestus passage follows similar lines, fundamental suspicions automatically arise.

Nevertheless, Orosius' understanding has stuck. E. Mary Smallwood, for example, has written recently that "the only reasonable interpretation of Suetonius' sentence is that the reference is to Christianity...."[19] Her single supporting evidence, however, is a reference to Arnaldo Momigliano's classic work on the Emperor Claudius. He wrote that "those who deny that the `Chrestus' of Suetonius is Christ must undertake the onus of proving their view...."[20] What evidence does Momigliano use to support his position? None, and this is typical for the subject as a whole, because for the very large number of scholars accepting Orosius' interpretation of the text, there is a very small amount of evidence sustaining that interpretation. Specifically, F.F. Bruce[21] provided more than most as has Gerd Luedemann[22] recently, while the classic work on this position remains Henri Janne's 1934 article.[23]

Consequently, the first task in dealing with the Chrestus passage is indeed one of demolition. Thus, the purpose of this study is simply to lay to rest the present scholarly consensus by gathering from the history of research each argument used in support of the Chrestus-Christus identification and then demonstrating its irrelevance or fallaciousness.

The most common of these arguments rests on evidence that the term Chrestus is an ancient alternative form of Christus. This looms so large

---

[14]Dio Cassius *Epitome* 67.14.1-2.

[15]*Hist. eccl.* 3.18.4.

[16]*Historiarum* 7.4.

[17]E. Schürer, *The History of the Jewish People in the Age of Jesus Christ* (ed. by G. Vermes and F. Millar; 3 vols.; Edinburgh: T. and T. Clark, 1973), vol. 3, pp. 163-4.

[18]*Historiarum* 7.6.

[19]Smallwood, p. 211.

[20]Momigliano, p. 33.

[21]F. F. Bruce, *Commentary on the Book of Acts* (1954; reprint ed., Grand Rapids: Wm. B. Eerdmans, 1966), p. 368; "Christianity under Claudius," *BJRL* 44 (1962), pp. 309-26.

[22]G. Luedemann, *Paul Apostle to the Gentiles: Studies in Chronology* (Philadelphia: Fortress Press, 1984), pp. 1-2, 6-7, 164-75.

[23]See n. 1.

because, unless Chrestus can mean Christus, there are no grounds whatsoever for associating the text in Suetonius with anything in Christianity. Hence, the error of Momigliano and Smallwood in asserting that the onus falls upon those who would deny a Christian interpretation, for such interpretation enters the realm of possibility only after demonstration that the person who wrote Chrestus *could* have meant Christus by that term. Unfortunately, the evidence is not conclusive here. Tacitus may well have written "chrestianos" in his *Annals* 15.44,[24] and the corresponding Greek spelling appears in Codex Sinaiticus.[25] Furthermore, both Tertullian[26] and Lactantius[27] complain of pagan mispronunciation along the same lines. Suetonius himself, however, in the one place where he made a clear reference to the new religion, called its adherents *christiani* rather than *chrestiani*,[28] a consideration which might lead to the conclusion that Suetonius saw no association between the previously mentioned Chrestus and the religion of the christianorum.[29] In any case, no such association is made by his texts, and the latter reads as if it were the first time Suetonius mentioned anything to do with the new movement.[30] Thus, in the case of Suetonius at least—and it is, after all, his meaning in question here—significant doubt exists concerning even the possibility of associating Chrestus with anything in Christianity. However, granted the vagaries of textual transmission, i.e., the possibility that *christiani* is no more than a scribal correction of what was perhaps Suetonius' original *chrestiani*, it is safest at this point not to rule out all together that Suetonius or his source could have used Chrestus for Christus.[31]

Nonetheless, granting the supposition that Suetonius could have meant Christus provides no support for the view that this is what he did mean, for Chrestus was an otherwise common Greco-Roman name.[32] Hence, Friedrich

---

[24]H. Fuchs, "Tacitus über die Christen," *VC* 4 (1950) 65.

[25]Acts 11:26, 26:28 and 1 Pet. 4:16.

[26]*Apology* 3.

[27]*Divine Institutes* 4.7.

[28]*Nero* 16.2.

[29]B. Baldwin, *Suetonius* (Amsterdam: Adolf M. Hakkert, 1983), p. 355.

[30]Graves and Podro, p. 40.

[31]Note, however, that Orosius (according to Janne [541 m. 4] a later scribe working on Orosius) performed the reverse process by changing Suetonius' Chrestus to Christus.

[32]See, for example, the large number of entries in the *Thesaurus linguae Latinae, Onomasticon* 2 (C); K. Linck, "De antiquissimis veterum quae ad Iesum Nazarenum spectant testimoniis," *Religionsgeschichtliche Versuche und Vorarbeiten* 14 (1913/1914), p. 106 m. 2; *Inscriptiones Latinae selectae* (ed. H. Dessau; 3 vols.;

Blass, to whom all modern scholars refer in support of the possibility that Chrestus may signify Christus, actually rejected this interpretation in the Suetonius passage: "Auf die bekannte Stelle des Suetonius Claud. 25...lege ich kein Gewicht, weil ich nicht einsehe, warum es nicht wirklich damals in Rom einen unruhigen Juden dieses Namens gegeben haben soll."[33]

Therefore, although Chrestus may perhaps mean Christus, it can just as or more easily refer to some other person of the same name. Alone and unsupported by something else within the context of the passage, no reason exists for making the Chrestus-Christus identification. By way of comparison, Suetonius *Nero* 16.2 is quite revealing: "Punishment was inflicted on the Christians [*christiani*], a class of men given to a new and mischievous superstition" (LCL). Even if this text read "chrestiani," there could be no doubt concerning its reference to Christianity because first, Chrestus is, but *chrestianus* is not, ambiguous; second, the context itself refers to a new, harmful religion; and third, there is a direct parallel in Tacitus. This also, in his *Annals* 15.44, deserves comparison with the Chrestus passage. Tacitus wrote concerning "a class of men, loathed for their vices, whom the crowd styled Christians. Christus, the founder of the name, had undergone the death penalty in the reign of Tiberius, by sentence of the procurator Pontius Pilatus..."[34] There can be no doubt here that the reference is to Christianity in Rome. The context makes it certain. Thus, the comparison of *Nero* 16.2 and *Annals* 15.44 with the Chrestus passage highlights the fact that the Christian interpretation of the former two is required while that of the latter is certainly not. Consequently, unless other evidence exists, there is no reason to associate the Chrestus passage with any aspect of Christianity.

The second argument commonly used in support of the Chrestus-Christus identification simply shows again where the real onus in the matter lies. Namely, Suetonius wrote that Chrestus was actually in Rome doing his instigating. But, when was Jesus in Rome? Hence, Janne argues that Chrestus really means Christianity.[35] That, however, is not what the text says. Graetz concludes that the reference is to the Christian apostle, Chrestus, mentioned by Paul in 1 Corinthians 1,[36] yet Paul mentions Christus, not Chrestus. Finally,

---

Berlin: Weidmannsche Verlagsbuchhandlung, 1962), vol. 1, pp. 1903A, 2156, 5247, 3004, 3549, 6073, 6740a, 7176, 7381, 7890, 7891, 8967.

[33]Blass, p. 467-8.

[34]This translation from the LCL does not take account of Fuchs' view (pp. 65, 69-70) that the preferred reading here is "chrestianos" rather than "christianos."

[35]Janne, p. 546.

[36]Graetz, pp. 202 and 231.

Robert Graves and Joshua Podro, assuming Chrestus to be Christus, i.e., Jesus Christ, use this text as their principal evidence for the view that Jesus actually escaped dying on the cross, went off to Rome and caused trouble there.[37] Since none of these is convincing, however, the normal route has been to conclude that either Suetonius or his source erred in thinking that Jesus was personally in Rome during the reign of Claudius. Thus, to posit a Christian interpretation it becomes necessary to fall back on a major error in the text and so conclude that Suetonius confused the one being preached with those who were preaching him.[38]

So, where does the onus really lie? In a passage the context of which provides no other obvious reason to assume it, a Chrestus appears who, among various Chresti of the Roman Empire, is supposed to be Jesus Christus and who, though this particular Christus never was in Rome, instigated riots in that city. Clearly, therefore, the onus rests upon those who support the Chrestus-Christus identification to provide grounds sufficient to overcome what are, in fact, major obstacles to such an interpretation. Unless this can be done, there is no reason whatsoever to associate the Chrestus passage with anything in early Christianity.

Thus, a great deal of attention has come to be focused on Acts 18:1-3 as if it did provide such evidence:

> After this he [Paul] left Athens and went to Corinth. And he found a Jew named Aquila, a native of Pontus, lately come from Italy with his wife Priscilla, because Claudius had commanded all the Jews to leave Rome....[39]

There can be little doubt that the *expulsion* of *Jews* from *Rome* by *Claudius* here and in Suetonius refers to the same event. Interestingly, Janne offers a free emendation in Acts so that Aquila is no longer a Jew but "a certain Christian,"[40] and Jewett provides another so that it was actually Christians rather than Jews

---

[37]Graves and Podro, p. 42.

[38]Among other scholars, this explanation appears in Janne (pp. 538 and 546), G. May ("La politique religieuse de l'Empereur Claude," *Revue historique de droit francais et étranger*, 4th ser. 17 [1938], p. 40), H. Leon (*The Jews of Ancient Rome* [Morris Loeb Series 5; Philadelphia: Jewish Publication Society of America, 1960], p. 26), E.M. Smallwood ("Jews and Romans in the Early Empire," *History Today* 15 [1965], p. 236), W. Wiefel ("Die jüdische Gemeinschaft im antiken Rom und die Anfänge des römischen Christentums," *Judaica* 26 [1970], p. 76) and Luedemann (p. 169).

[39]RSV.

[40]Janne, p. 536.

expelled from Rome.[41] Granted that this sounds very much like Eusebius at work on Flavia Domitilla or Orosius on Helena of Adiabene, there is in fact some evidence to support Janne's view that Aquila was a Christian on his arrival in Corinth. Specifically, though Acts simply calls him a Jew from Pontus, Aquila soon appears active as Paul's co-worker in the gospel. Since Acts, however, does not report his conversion, Janne,[42] K. Lake - H.J. Cadbury[43] and F.F. Bruce[44] take this to mean he was already a Christian on arrival in Corinth from Rome. Additional evidence for this view is then provided from Acts in that Paul and Aquila would never have joined together in a common trade had they not shared the same gospel.[45]

In spite of these arguments, however, the clear sense of Acts is that Aquila was not a Christian when he arrived in Corinth from Rome. First, Acts states specifically that he was a Jew.[46] Second, it also states that the original bond between Aquila and Paul was professional. They shared the same trade, not the same religion. Third, the order in Acts (a Jew from Pontus, a co-worker with Paul in the leather trade, a Christian missionary) certainly appears intended by the author of Acts to show a progression from Jew to Christian through instrumental contact with Paul. Thus, Acts can be used only to provide evidence for exactly what it says, namely, that Aquila was a Jew from Pontus expelled with all other Jews from Rome.[47] As for Jewett's emendation, it has no value because it takes the point to be proven and makes it a presupposition. And again, Acts says that it was Jews who were expelled. Perhaps pagan writers might easily have confused the two groups. The author of Acts did not.

Moreover, nothing would really be proven if Aquila had been a Christian in Rome at the time of the expulsion, for if he was a Christian, he was a Jewish Christian, i.e., a Jew from Pontus living in Rome who thought Jesus to be the

---

[41]R. Jewett, *A Chronology of Paul's Life* (Philadelphia: Fortress Press, 1979), p. 36.

[42]Janne, p. 536 m. 1.

[43]K. Lake and H. J. Cadbury, *The Beginnings of Christianity* (5 vols.; London: Macmillan and Co., 1933), vol. 4, p. 222.

[44]Bruce, "Christianity," p. 316.

[45]Wiefel, p. 77, Luedemann, p. 174.

[46]This is also how Eusebius reads the passage in Acts.

[47]Janne (p. 539) is certainly correct that the author of Acts was not likely to want to draw attention to Christian-related disturbances in Rome, but he fails to recognize the real implication of this view. Namely, had the writer of Acts thought these events associated in any way with Christianity, he simply would have omitted all reference to them.

messiah. Even without the text of Acts, however, it is necessary to assume that the expulsion of Jews from Rome included those with zealot leanings, any favorably disposed toward Qumran, probably Samaritans, Pharisees, the *ammei haaretz*, perhaps supporters of the claims of Simon Magus, and Jews who were sympathetic toward Jesus, provided such were in Rome by the time of the event described in Suetonius.[48] The common denominator in all of these cases is that the persons included are Jews, just as in Suetonius, Acts and Eusebius—as well as in Dio Cassius and Orosius for that matter—the common denominator is Judaism.[49] No amount of wishful thinking or free emendation can change that. Hence, under no circumstances whatsoever does Acts 18:1-3 lend support to the Christian interpretation of the Suetonius passage.

Another argument associated with Acts focuses on the parallel drawn by scholars between a series of events described in Acts and what occurred in the Suetonius passage. Thus, it happens very often in this New Testament text that when Paul arrives in a city to preach the gospel, he is soon met by very hostile Jewish actions which end up in riots (Antioch, 13:44-50; Iconium, 14:1-7; Lystra, 14:19; Thessalonica, 17:5-9; Beroea, 17:13; Corinth, 18:5-6, 12-17; etc.) Hence, Smallwood argues by way of analogy that this same thing must have occurred in Rome when the gospel was first preached in the Jewish community there.[50] Namely, the unresponsive Jews, that violent lot portrayed in Acts, rioted at the appearance of the preaching of the gospel concerning Jesus, i.e., "impulsore Chresto."

This position also, however, is not convincing. In the first place, it depends entirely upon the credibility of Acts, but Acts tends to slander non-Christian Jews as rabble-rousers, troublemakers, disturbers of the peace and would-be murderers. Hence, the constantly repeated image of the Jewish rabble-rousers instigating the crowds at the appearance of Paul is a creation of Acts based on an anti-Jewish topos in other Greco-Roman literature. It is not possible, therefore, to draw historical analogies from it.[51] Thus, second, there is no reason to think that the introduction of the gospel into the Roman Jewish community produced the tumults mentioned by Suetonius. Finally, and most important, other early Jewish difficulties in Rome were not associated with Christianity. If Valerius

---

[48]So, for example, E. Bammel, "Judenverfolgung und Näherwartung: Zur Eschatologie des Ersten Thessalonicherbriefs," *ZTK* 56 (1959), p. 300.

[49]Linck, p. 105.

[50]Smallwood, *The Jews*, p. 212; also, May, p. 39, m. 2 and Bruce, "Christianity," p. 322.

[51]D. Slingerland, "'The Jews' in the Pauline Portion of Acts," *Journal of the American Academy of Religion* 54 (1986), pp. 305-21.

Maximus is to be trusted, Jews had already been expelled from Rome as early as 139 B.C.E. and this, obviously, unassociated with things Christian. The charge was corrupting Roman customs.[52] Again, Cicero claimed to have been very fearful of the political power of Roman Jews.[53] And in 19 C.E., Tiberius expelled them from Rome for uncertain reasons, but, in any case, reasons not associated with Christianity.[54] Historical analogy alone, therefore, makes clear that it is entirely unnecessary to posit Christian causes for the expulsion under Claudius.[55]

Thus, nothing in the evidence so far presented supports the Christian interpretation of Suetonius *Claudius* 25.4. That evidence has either been irrelevant, fallacious or supportive of the opposite conclusion. It remains only, therefore, to discuss the last few arguments in defense of the Chrestus-Christus identification.

The most popular of these is the one proposed originally by Janne that if Chrestus had been some unknown person, Suetonius would have written "Chresto quodam," "a certain Chrestus." Since he did not, he must have had Jesus in mind.[56] As K. Linck pointed out even prior to Janne, however, the identity of Chrestus is a modern puzzle: nothing permits the assumption of Suetonius' ignorance in this matter.[57] Hence, the absence of the quodam, if it means anything at all, simply shows that Suetonius had a particular Chrestus in mind but in no way implies this to have been Jesus.[58]

Janne runs into even more problems in arguing that Suetonius' term *assidue* (constantly) characterizes the nature of Christian preaching in Rome.[59] In the first place, it is the Jewish response to the instigation (*assidue tumultuantes*) rather than the instigation itself which is described by the adverb. Second, there is nothing characteristically Christian about this particular term. Nonetheless, convinced that the events portrayed in Suetonius and Dio Cassius represent the

[52]Valerius Maximus, *Factorum ac dictorum memorabilium libri, Epitome* 1.3.3.

[53]Cicero *Pro Flacco* 66-68.

[54]Josephus *Ant.* 18.65-84; Tacitus *Annals* 2.85; Suetonius *Tiberius* 36.

[55]Benko, p. 412.

[56]Janne, pp. 540-41; so, also, for example, Graves and Podro, p. 39; Bruce, *Commentary*, p. 368.

[57]Linck, p. 106.

[58]B. Baldwin (p. 356) doubts that Suetonius would have recognized some otherwise unknown Chrestus. Again, however, modern readers have no way of gauging what was Suetonius' common knowledge.

[59]Janne, pp. 544 and 547.

same occurrence,[60] Janne goes on to claim that several further items characteristic of Christianity appear in the words of Dio's account (60.6.6):

> As for the Jews...he did not drive them out, but ordered them...not to hold meetings. He also disbanded the clubs [*hetaireias*], which had been reintroduced by Gaius. Moreover...he abolished the taverns where they [the Roman populace] were wont to gather and drink, and commanded that no boiled meat or hot water should be sold....(LCL)

According to Janne, this passage makes specific reference to Christian *hetaireias* and meals and so, like *assidue* in Suetonius, supports the Chrestus-Christus identification in *Claudius* 25.4.[61] In fact, however, the introduction of Dio Cassius' text only raises new problems for the Christian interpretation without providing it with any additional support. First, it raises the very difficult question of whether Suetonius and Dio Cassius referred to the same event. That issue remains unresolved. Second, if they did, Janne has actually complicated his own task. To be specific, Suetonius provides no date for the expulsion associated with Chrestus. Thus, it may have happened any time during the 41 to 54 C.E. reign of Claudius. Dio Cassius, however, did imply a date in the first year of that emperor, and this necessarily raises the question of when Christianity reached Rome. Could it be shown, for example, that the arrival occurred after 54 C.E., it would be impossible to defend the association between Chrestus and Christus. However, Paul's ca. 58 C.E. letter to a well established community in Rome makes it very likely that the church had already existed there for some time. Nonetheless, since earlier, trustworthy *termini ante quem* for the arrival of Christianity in Rome do not exist, there is no way to determine exactly when that took place.[62] The only certain thing is that the earlier the date of the Chrestus event, the less likely it involved Christianity.[63] Thus, Janne's association of this event with Dio Cassius and 41 C.E. requires the very early introduction and significant development of the new religion in the capital of the empire.[64] Such a date may not be impossible, but it is certainly far less likely than one later in the reign of Claudius.

---

[60]Ibid., pp. 533-34.

[61]Ibid., pp. 548-50.

[62]Contrary to Janne, p. 547.

[63]This is especially so since the first evidence of Roman ability to recognize the new religion in the capital appears in Tacitus' account (*Annals* 15.44) of events associated with 64 C.E.

[64]On the basis of the description in Acts 28 of Paul's arrival in Rome, Borg (p. 212) argues that as late as that event the Jewish community was hardly aware of Christianity. Janne (p. 540) is no doubt correct, however, that Acts intentionally played down pre-Pauline Jewish Christianity in Rome in order to make Paul's role

Third, and more specifically, there is nothing in Dio Cassius' passage even hinting of Christianity. According to Dio himself the clubs disbanded by Claudius had been closed previously by Tiberius, i.e., reintroduced by his successor Gaius. Hence, they were typical, pre-Christian, social-political organizations. Again, terms such as "tavern," "boiled meat" and "hot water" do bring to mind meals but hardly the kind, or at least not specifically the kind, associated with early Christian fellowship. Furthermore, it appears here that Dio was referring to similar but distinctive actions against three unrelated entities, i.e., Jewish meetings, clubs and taverns. Most important, and related to this last, Dio Cassius, like Suetonius, though certainly knowledgeable about Christianity, singled out the Jewish community as the focus of Claudius' action. This particular form of argumentation, therefore, rather than supporting the Chrestus-Christus identification, actually makes it less likely.

All that remain in support of the Christian interpretation of Claudius 25.4 are two arguments *e silentio*. One depends upon the fact that Josephus, who tended to avoid the mention of things Christian, failed to recount the expulsion noted by Suetonius. In light of this, Janne concludes that the historian must have omitted the Chrestus event in order to pass over in silence a reference to the new religion.[65] Like other arguments of the same type, however, the present one is not convincing. Most obviously, it means that any event known from other writers but omitted by Josephus may have been Christian related. More important, the fact of the Jewish expulsion is itself cause enough to explain why Josephus, a Roman Jew and imperial apologist for his people, should have chosen to pass over any reference to such an event. This is especially likely in that he had already found it necessary to describe and explain away the earlier expulsion of Roman Jews under Tiberius.[66] Hence, if anything may be made of Josephus' silence, it is that Claudius did indeed expel Jews from Rome. In any case, nothing in his omission leads to the conclusion of Christian involvement in the Chrestus event.

The other argument *e silentio* was proposed recently by Gerd Luedemann. He has two goals, first, to demonstrate that Suetonius and Dio Cassius were dependent upon a common source for their descriptions of Claudius' punitive action against Roman Jews, and, second, to show that the Jewish disorders were Christian instigated. As Luedemann recognizes, however, the difficulty with the

---

more significant. After all, Paul wrote his letter to a substantial Christian community in Rome *prior* to his visit there. Hence, Acts 28 has no bearing on when the gospel concerning Jesus took root in the capital.

[65] Janne, p. 551.

[66] Josephus *Ant.* 18.65-84.

latter position is that Dio wrote not a word about Christian involvement in these disorders. Nonetheless, he is able to explain this in exactly the same way Janne had handled Josephus. That is, like Josephus, Dio tended to avoid reference to Christianity. Therefore, Dio's silence about this part of the Roman disturbances simply confirms that Christianity did appear as their cause in the source used jointly by Dio and Suetonius. Thus, since Suetonius in turn used this source, his reference to Chrestus must actually be to Christus, i.e., to things Christian.[67] Luedemann is of course guilty of the same fundamental weakness as Janne in that on the basis of the absence of reference he posits the presence of reference and so expects readers to believe that Dio Cassius, who is explicit about the purely Jewish nature of the described events, really supports the Christian interpretation of these happenings.

Thus, the demolition is complete. Arguments used in support of the Chrestus-Christus identification in Suetonius *Claudius* 25.4 turn out to be either irrelevant or fallacious and often to support the position they were intended to deny. That is, the Chrestus event makes perfectly good sense just as it appears in Suetonius, Acts and, provided he was referring to the same occurrence, Dio Cassius. Namely, it was a significant happening within the history of early Roman Jewry, one worthy of examination for its own sake and in no way a candidate for Christian baptism.

---

[67]Luedemann, pp. 166 m. 76, 169.

Index to Biblical and Rabbinic Sources

General Index

Albeck, H., 15, 37, 39, 49, 52, 55, 69, 75

Alfasi, Isaac, 3

Alon, G., 125, 126

Aristotle, economics, 83, 84f., 95

Ashi, and Talmudic redaction, 34, 73, 80

Augustine, utopian program, 84

Avery-Peck, A., 103

Bacher, W., 5, 6

Baldwin, B., 136, 141

Bammel, E., 140

Baron, S., 3, 5, 90ff.

Bavli, relationship to Yerushalmi, 3ff., 23

Bell, R, 128

Benko, S., 133, 141

Blass, F., 134, 137

Bokser, B., 4, 15

Borg, M., 133

Bornkamm, G, 134

Brooks, R, 85, 103

Bruce, F.F., 135, 139

Brüll, N., 48,

Büchler, A., 126

Cadbury, H.J., 139

Charlesworth, J.M., 130

Christianity, theory of economy, 95

Cohen, A., 77

Danielou, J., 131

Davadide ruler, 9ff.

Davis, J., 4

DeVries, B., 37

Diverse-kinds, and gentile, 111ff., grafting, 116, in Scripture, 111, outside of Israel, 117, working, 117

Douglas, M., 111

Dowry, doubling amount of, 30f.

Economics, and social system, 94

Eddy, S., 126, 127, 128

Efrati, Y., 49

Eilberg-Schwartz, H., 103

Eisler, R., 133

Epstein, J.N., 5, 69, 75

Expiation offering, 10ff.

Feldblum, M., 48, 77

Feliks, J., 117

Fox-Genovese, E, 83

Frankel, Z., 52

Friedman, M., 48

Friedman, S., 29, 30, 35, 48, 49, 50, 55, 59, 78

Fuchs, H., 136f.

Gaster, T., 130

Gemara, Apodictic style, 44, 74, infixes, 58ff., straw-man arguments, 54ff., 63ff.

Ginzberg, L., 3, 5

Goldberg, A., 52

Goodblatt, D., 3, 4, 6, 38

Graetz, H., 133, 137

Graves, R., 133, 136f.

Gross, N., 92, 93

Gulak, A., 124, 131

Hadas, M., 126, 127

Hai Gaon, 3

Halevy, I., 39

Hellenism, in Palestine, 126ff.

149